TWO IN ONE

Selected Poems

and

The Frog Prince
and other poems

TWO IN ONE

Selected Poems
and
The Frog Prince
and other poems

by Stevie Smith.

LONGMAN

LONGMAN GROUP LIMITED
LONDON

*Associated companies, branches and representatives
throughout the world*

© Stevie Smith 1962 and 1966

This double volume first published 1971

This edition first published 1971

ISBN 0 582 12770 X (case)
ISBN 0 582 12771 8 (paper)

*Printed in Great Britain by
Lowe & Brydone (Printers) Ltd., London*

CONTENTS

v

xi

ACKNOWLEDGEMENTS

Selected Poems

We are grateful to Chapman & Hall for permission to include the following poems from their publication *Harold's Leap* by Stevie Smith: The Roman Road; Behind the Knight; Harold's Leap; The Weak Monk; The Ambassador; Le Singe Qui Swing; The Afterthought; The Warden; The Death Sentence; Pad, Pad; The Deserter; Thought is Superior; The Orphan Reformed; Cool and Plain; The Wanderer; The River God; My Cats; Oh Stubborn Race of Cadmus' Seed, and Andre Deutsch Ltd. for the following poems from *Not Waving But Drowning* by Stevie Smith: Not Waving But Drowning; The Old Sweet Dove of Wiveton; The Blue from Heaven; 'Come On, Come Back'; Away, Melancholy; In the Park; Fafnir and the Knights; The Airy Christ; The Jungle Husband; I Remember; The Singing Cat; Parents; Songe d'Athalie; The Starling; Childe Rolandine; The Fairy Bell; Why are the Clergy . . . ?; The Queen and the Young Princess; Longing for Death because of Feebleness; Loin de l'Etre.

The Frog Prince & other Poems

We are grateful to Chapman & Hall Ltd for permission to include the following poems from their publication *Harold's Leap* by Stevie Smith: The Castle; Touch and Go; Man is a Spirit; Do Take Muriel Out; The Broken Friendship; I rode with my darling; Mr Over; God and Man; Our Bog is Dood; The Rehearsal; The Hat; Voices about the Princess Anemone; Wretched Woman; Lightly Bound; and to André Deutsch for the following poems from *Not Waving But Drowning* by Stevie Smith: St. Anthony and the Rose of Life; Anger's Freeing Power; At School; The Occasional Yarrow; Who is this Who Howls and Mutters?; Will Man Ever Face Fact and not Feel Flat?; A Dream of Comparison; A Dream of Nourishment; Oh What is the Thing He Done?; The Choosers; But Murderous; and to Gaberbocchus for the following poems from *Some are More Human than Others* by Stevie Smith: Everything is Swimming; The Persian; Lord Say-and-Seal.

xiii

SELECTED POEMS

Thoughts about the Person from Porlock

COLERIDGE received the Person from Porlock
And ever after called him a curse,
Then why did he hurry to let him in?
He could have hid in the house.

It was not right of Coleridge in fact it was wrong
(But often we all do wrong)
As the truth is I think he was already stuck
With Kubla Khan.

He was weeping and wailing: I am finished, finished,
I shall never write another word of it,
When along comes the Person from Porlock
And takes the blame for it.

It was not right, it was wrong,
But often we all do wrong.

May we enquire the name of the Person from Porlock?
Why, Porson, didn't you know?
He lived at the bottom of Porlock Hill
So had a long way to go,

He wasn't much in the social sense
Though his grandmother was a Warlock,
One of the Rutlandshire ones I fancy
And nothing to do with Porlock,

And he lived at the bottom of the hill as I said
And had a cat named Flo,
And had a cat named Flo.

Thoughts about the Person from Porlock (*contd.*)

I long for the Person from Porlock
To bring my thoughts to an end,
I am becoming impatient to see him
I think of him as a friend,

2

Often I look out of the window
Often I run to the gate
I think, He will come this evening,
I think it is rather late.

I am hungry to be interrupted
For ever and ever amen
O Person from Porlock come quickly
And bring my thoughts to an end.

I felicitate the people who have a Person from Porlock
To break up everything and throw it away
Because then there will be nothing to keep them
And they need not stay.

Why do they grumble so much?
He comes like a benison
They should be glad he has not forgotten them
They might have had to go on.

These thoughts are depressing I know.   They are
    depressing,
I wish I was more cheerful, it is more pleasant,
Also it is a duty, we should smile as well as submitting
To the purpose of One Above who is experimenting
With various mixtures of human character which goes
    best,
All is interesting for him it is exciting, but not for us.
There I go again.   Smile, smile, and get some work
    to do
Then you will be practically unconscious without
    positively having to go.

Thoughts about the Christian Doctrine of Eternal Hell

Is it not interesting to see
How the Christians continually
Try to separate themselves in vain
From the doctrine of eternal pain.

They cannot do it,
They are committed to it,
Their Lord said it,
They must believe it.

So the vulnerable body is stretched without pity
On flames for ever.   Is this not pretty?

The religion of Christianity
Is mixed of sweetness and cruelty
Reject this Sweetness, for she wears
A smoky dress out of hell fires.

4

Who makes a God? Who shows him thus?
It is the Christian religion does,
Oh, oh, have none of it,
Blow it away, have done with it.

This god the Christians show
Out with him, out with him, let him go.

Recognition not Enough

SIN recognised—but that—may keep us humble,
But oh, it keeps us nasty.

Was He Married?

WAS he married, did he try
    To support as he grew less fond of them
Wife and family?

No,
He never suffered such a blow.

Did he feel pointless, feeble and distrait,
Unwanted by everyone and in the way?

From his cradle he was purposeful,
His bent strong and his mind full.

Did he love people very much
Yet find them die one day?

He did not love in the human way.

Did he ask how long it would go on,
Wonder if Death could be counted on for an end?

He did not feel like this,
He had a future of bliss.

Did he never feel strong
Pain for being wrong?

He was not wrong, he was right,
He suffered from others', not his own, spite.

But there *is* no suffering like having made a mistake
Because of being of an inferior make.

He was not inferior,
He was superior.

He knew then that power corrupts but some must
    govern?

His thoughts were different.

Did he lack friends?   Worse,
Think it was for his fault, not theirs?

He did not lack friends,
He had disciples he moulded to his ends.

Did he feel over-handicapped sometimes, yet must
    draw even?

How could he feel like this?   He was the King of
    Heaven.

. . . find a sudden brightness one day in everything
Because a mood had been conquered, or a sin?

I tell you, he did not sin.

Do only human beings suffer from the irritation
I have mentioned?   learn too that being comical
Does not ameliorate the desperation?

Only human beings feel this,
It is because they are so mixed.

All human beings should have a medal,
A god cannot carry it, he is not able.

A god is Man's doll, you ass,
He makes him up like this on purpose.

He might have made him up worse.

He often has, in the past.

To choose a god of love, as he did and does,
Is a little move then?

Yes, it is.

A larger one will be when men
Love love and hate hate but do not deify them?

It will be a larger one.

Was it not curious?

W<small>AS</small> it not curious of Aúgustin
    Saint Aúgustin, Saint Aúgustin,
When he saw the beautiful British children
To say such a curious thing?

He said he must send the gospel, the gospel,
At once to them over the waves
He never said he thought it was wicked
To steal them away for slaves

To steal the children away
To buy and have slavery at all
Oh no, oh no, it was not a thing
That caused him any appal.

Was it not curious of *Gregory*
Rather more than of Aúgustin?
It was not curious so much
As it was wicked of them.

The Frozen Lake

To a mere
    Sir Bedevere
Consigned Excalibur.

White and silent is the snowflake
Falling falling, and it will make
Soon all flat and like a white lake
In a white and silent state
Beaming flat and vacant.

Underneath the frozen water
Steps the Lord of Ullan's daughter
She is a witch of endless might
And rules the borders of the night.

So however white and silent
Seems the lake, it is not vacant
But contains Lord Ullan's daughter
Walking as her Uncle taught her.

Her Uncle is a greater sage
At witchcraft than the lady is
But he has gone, one knows not where
And so his niece only is here.

No, this water is not vacant
But is full of deep intent
Of deep intent and management
Contrived by Ullan's daughter
To what end I know not.

And to my mind the lake is brighter
For the lady's presence; whiter
Though its coat of winter make it
It is for Ullan's daughter's sake it
Beams to me so brightly.

Often as I gaze upon it
Tread upon the ice upon it
I can feel the water shiver
As the lady with a slither
Comes to tap the ice, to tear it,
Yes, I think that I can hear it
Tapped and tickled with her fingers
Where a floe in splinter lingers
Where I cannot come.
But I swear I hear her, seem to
See her face that seems to beam to
Me that hovers half-enchanted
Yes I hover half-enchanted
Wondering if I am wanted
Beckoned by her smile or threatened,
And as always, so today
As I stand and wonder, Ullan's daughter
Goes away.

To a mere
Sir Bedevere
Consigned Excalibur
And who is this who now comes here?
It *is* Sir Bedevere.

This afternoon Sir Bedevere
Found me hesitating by
The icy lake, and he said: Sir,
Where lies the sword Excalibur?

I answered with a lie:
'It must be in some other mere.'
And then I said, 'I truly love her,
Love the Lord of Ullan's daughter
And so I answered with a lie
As I can only think of her.
Oh shall I go beneath the water
Where she walks, or wait for her?
Tell me, Sir Bedevere,
Shall I wait here for her?
H looked at me, but did not say
A word, then he too went away.

And so they go.   I am alone,
The white lake beams beneath the moon,
O dear white lake, O dearest love
That will not show yourself above
The bitter ice, but leave me here
To be annoyed by Bedevere,
I come, I come.   And then I dived
Into the lake, but through my side
As I went down to seek for her
There passed the sword Excalibur,
In cold and silence seek for her,
The sword sunk in the mere.

And so I died, and the lake-water
That holds the form of Ullan's daughter
With all my blood is dyed,
Is dyed,
With all my love is dyed.

Poor Soul, poor Girl!

(A DEBUTANTE)

I CANNOT imagine anything nicer
  Than to be struck by lightning and killed suddenly
    crossing a field
As if somebody cared.
Nobody cares whether I am alive or dead.

From the French

INDOLENT youth,
  Drawn by everything in turn,
By not being decided enough
I lost my life.

Admire Cranmer!

ADMIRE the old man, admire him, admire him,
Mocked by the priests of Mary Tudor, given to the flames,
Flinching and overcoming the flinching, Cranmer.

Admire the martyrs of Bloody Mary's reign,
In the shocking arithmetic of cruel average, ninety
A year, three-hundred; admire them.

But still I cry: Admire the Archbishop,
The old man, the scholar, admire him.
Not simply, for flinching and overcoming simply,
But for his genius, admire him,
His delicate feelings of genius, admire him,

That wrote the Prayer Book
(Admire him!)
And made the flames burn crueller.   Admire Cranmer!

Votaries of Both Sexes Cry First to Venus

Crying for pleasure,
Crying for pain,
Longing to see you
Again and again.

To the tune:
Angels of Jesus,
Angels of light
Singing to welcome
The pilgrims of the night.
(from Hymns A. & M.)

But one stood up and said: I love
The love that comes in the dark fields,
In the late night, in the hot breathless dark night;
In the moony forest, when there is a moon,
In the moony rides of the dark forest.

I love this love; it is eerie if there is not
My love in *my* arms then.   It is an excitement
In the arms of a person.   It is exciting then,
It is such an excitement as is on the approach
Of Death; it is *my* love in *my* arms, and then
The trees and the dark trees and the soft grass and the moon
Are not arrogant, as they are if I am alone,
Not a measure, a great measure of indifference, not arrogant
Or in their way exciting either in a way that is too much.

Here this person standing up before Venus wept
And wept, and the tears of this person were warm
And this person then said: There is no love in my arms
No sweet person I love in my arms, and the tears
And the soft strong feelings I parade underneath the trees,
I lay them down; on the soft dark grass I lay down
My strong feelings.   They are for you to eat up, Venus,
But you do not care for them much.   Then they are
For the god who created me.   Let him have them.

Then this person began to laugh and to dance
And Venus was offended; but behind Venus there came
First a little light, then some laughter, then a hand
That took up the great feelings, and then a blessing fell
Like the moon, and there was not any Venus any longer
But the votaries were not abashed, they were blessed

> Crying for pleasure,   (*tune as above*)
> Crying for pain,
> Longing to see you
> Again and again.

Yes this time when they sang their song they were blessed.

Not Waving but Drowning

NOBODY heard him, the dead man,
  But still he lay moaning:
I was much further out than you thought
And not waving but drowning.

Poor chap, he always loved larking
And now he's dead
It must have been too cold for him his **heart**
    gave way,
They said.

Oh, no no no, it was too cold always
(Still the dead one lay moaning)
I was much too far out all my life
And not waving but drowning.

From the French

"WE shall never be one mummy only
  Beneath the antique deserts and the happy **palms.**"

18

I *Was so Full* . . .

I WAS so full of love and joy
There was not enough people to love,
So I said: Let there be God,
Then there was God above.

I was so full of anger and hate
To be hated was not enough people,
So I said: Let there be a Devil to hate,
Then down below was the Devil.

These persons have worked very much in my mind
And by being not true, have made me unkind,
So now I say: Away with them, away; we should
Not believe fairy stories if we wish to be good.

Think of them as persons from the fairy wood.

The Old Sweet Dove of Wiveton

'TWAS the voice of the sweet dove
   I heard him move
I heard him cry
Love, love.

High in the chestnut tree
Is the nest of the old dove
And there he sits solitary
Crying, Love, love.

The gray of this heavy day
Makes the green of the trees' leaves and the grass
   brighter
And the flowers of the chestnut tree whiter
And whiter the flowers of the high cow-parsley.

20

So still is the air
So heavy the sky
You can hear the splash
Of the water falling from the green grass
As Red and Honey push by,
The old dogs,
Gone away, gone hunting by the marsh bogs.

Happy the retriever dogs in their pursuit
Happy in bog-mud the busy foot.

Now all is silent, it is silent again
In the sombre day and the beginning soft rain
It is a silence made more actual
By the moan from the high tree that is occasional,

Where in his nest above
Still sits the old dove,
Murmuring solitary
Crying for pain,
Crying most melancholy
Again and again.

From the Italian

(An Old Superstition)

A WOOLLY dog,
A red-haired man,
Better dead
Than to have met 'em.

God Speaks

I MADE Man with too many faults.   Yet I love him.
And if he wishes, I have a home above for him.
I should like him to be happy.   I am genial.
He should not paint me as if I were abominable.
As for instance, that I had a son and gave him for their
salvation.
This is one of the faults I meant.   It leads to nervous
prostration.
All the same, there is a difficulty.   I should like him to be
happy in heaven here,
But he cannot come by wishing.   Only by being already at
home here.

The Blue from Heaven

(A LEGEND OF KING ARTHUR OF BRITAIN)

KING ARTHUR rode in another world
And his twelve knights rode behind him
And Guinevere was there
Crying: Arthur, where are you dear?

Why is the King so blue
Why is he this blue colour?
It is because the sun is shining
And he rides under the blue cornflowers.

High wave the cornflowers
That shed the pale blue light
And under the tall cornflowers
Rides King Arthur and his twelve knights.

And Guinevere is there
Crying: Arthur, where are you dear?

First there were twelve knights riding
And then there was only one
And King Arthur said to the one knight,
Be gone.

All I wish for now, said Arthur,
Is the beautiful colour blue
And to ride in the blue sunshine
And Guinevere I do not wish for you.

Oh Lord, said Guinevere
I do not see the colour blue
And I wish to ride where our knights rode,
After you.

Go back, go back, Guinevere,
Go back to the palace, said the King.
So she went back to the palace
And her grief did not seem to her a small thing.

The Queen has returned to the palace
Crying: Arthur, where are you dear?
And everyday she speaks of Arthur's grandeur
To the knights who are there.

That Arthur has fallen from the grandeur
Of his powers all agree
And the falling off of Arthur
Becomes their theme presently.

As if it were only temporarily
And it was not for ever
They speak, but the Queen knows
He will come back never.

Yes, Arthur has passed away
Gladly he has laid down his reigning powers
He has gone to ride in the blue light
Of the peculiar towering cornflowers.

'Come on, Come back'

(*incident in a future war*)

LEFT by the ebbing tide of battle
On the field of Austerlitz
The girl soldier Vaudevue sits
Her fingers tap the ground, she is alone
At midnight in the moonlight she is sitting alone on a
    round flat stone

Graded by the Memel Conference first
Of all humane exterminators
M.L.5.
Has left her just alive
Only her memory is dead for evermore.
She fears and cries, Ah me why am I here?
Sitting alone on a round flat stone on a hummock there.

Rising, staggering, over the ground she goes
Over the seeming miles of rutted meadow
To the margin of a lake
The sand beneath her feet
Is cold and damp and firm to the waves' beat.

Quickly—as a child, an idiot, as one without memory—
She strips her uniform off, strips, stands and plunges
Into the icy waters of the adorable lake.
On the surface of the water lies
A ribbon of white moonlight
The waters on either side of the moony track
Are black as her mind.
Her mind is as secret from her
As the water on which she swims,
As secret as profound as ominous.

Weeping bitterly for her ominous mind, her plight
Up the river of white moonlight she swims
Until a treacherous undercurrent
Seizing her in an icy-amorous embrace
Dives with her, swiftly severing
The waters which close above her head.

An enemy sentinel
Finding the abandoned clothes
Waits for the swimmer's return
('Come on, come back')
Waiting, whiling away the hour
Whittling a shepherd's pipe from the hollow reeds.

In the chill light of dawn
Ring out the pipe's wild notes
'Come on, come back.'

Vaudevue
In the swift and subtle current's close embrace
Sleeps on, stirs not, hears not the familiar tune
Favourite of all the troops of all the armies
Favourite of Vaudevue
For she had sung it too
Marching to Austerlitz,
'Come on, come back.'

Away, Melancholy

AWAY, melancholy,
Away with it, let it go.

Are not the trees green,
The earth as green?
Does not the wind blow,
Fire leap and the rivers flow?
Away melancholy.

The ant is busy
He carrieth his meat,
All things hurry
To be eaten or eat.
Away, melancholy.

Man, too, hurries,
Eats, couples, buries,
He is an animal also
With a hey ho melancholy,
Away with it, let it go.

Man of all creatures
Is superlative
(Away melancholy)
He of all creatures alone
Raiseth a stone
(Away melancholy)
Into the stone, the god,
Pours what he knows of good
Calling good, God.
Away melancholy, let it go.

Speak not to me of tears,
Tyranny, pox, wars,
Saying, Can God
Stone of man s thought, be good?

Say rather it is enough
That the stuffed
Stone of man's good, growing,
By man's called God.
Away, melancholy, let it go.

Man aspires
To good,
To love
Sighs;

Beaten, corrupted, dying
In his own blood lying
Yet heaves up an eye above
Cries, Love, love.
It is his virtue needs explaining,
Not his failing.

Away, melancholy,
Away with it, let it go.

In the Park

WALKING one day in the park in winter
I heard two silvered gentlemen talking,
Two old friends, elderly, walking, talking
There by the silver lake mid-pooled black in winter.

'Pray for the Mute who have no word to say,'
Cried the one old gentleman, 'Not because they are dumb,
But they are weak.   And the weak thoughts beating in the
    brain
Generate a sort of heat, yet cannot speak.
Thoughts that are bound without sound
In the tomb of the brain's room, wound.   Pray for the Mute.'

'But' (said his friend), 'see how they swim
Free in the element best loved, so wet; yet breathe
As a visitor to the air come; plunge then, rejoicing more,
Having left it briefly for the visited shore, to come
Home to the wet
Windings that are yet
Best loved though familiar; and oh so right the wet
Stream and the wave; he is their pet.'

Finished, the mild friend
Smiled, put aside his well-tuned hearing instrument
And it seemed
The happiness he spoke of
Irradiated all his members, and his heart
Barked with delight to stress
So much another's happiness.

But which other's?   The sombre first
Speaker reversed
The happy moment; cried again
(Mousing for pain) 'Pray for the Mute' (a tear drops)
'They are like the brute.'

Struck by the shout
That he may not know what it's about
The deaf friend again
Up-ends his hearing instrument ₋o relieve the strain.
What? Oh shock, ' "Pray for the Mute"?
I thought you said the newt.'

Now which is Christianer pray, of these old friends, the one
    who will say
For pain's sake pray, pray; or the deaf other that rejoices
So much that the cool amphibian
Shall have his happiness, all things rejoicing with him?

But wait: the first speaker now, the old sombre one,
Is penetrated quite by his friend's sun
And, 'Oh blessed you,' he cries, 'to show
So in simplicity what is true.'
All his face is suffused with happy tears and as he weeps he
    sings a happy song,
Happier even than his friend's song was, righting the wrong.
So two, better than one, finally strike truth in this happy song:

'Praise,' cries the weeping softened one, 'Not pray, praise, all
    men,
Praise is the best prayer, the least self's there, that least's
    release.'

Fafnir and the Knights

IN the quiet waters
Of the forest pool
Fafnir the dragon
His tongue will cool

His tongue will cool
And his muzzle dip
Until the soft waters lave
His muzzle tip

Happy simple creature
In his coat of mail
With a mild bright eye
And a waving tail

Happy the dragon
In the days expended
Before the time had come for dragons
To be hounded

Delivered in their simplicity
To the Knights of the Advancing Band
Who seeing the simple dragon
Must kill him out of hand

The time has not come yet
But must come soon
Meanwhile happy Fafnir
Take thy rest in the afternoon

Take thy rest
Fafnir while thou mayest
In the long grass
Where thou liest

Happy knowing not
In thy simplicity
That the knights have come
To do away with thee.

When thy body shall be torn
And thy lofty spirit
Broken into pieces
For a knight's merit

When thy lifeblood shall be spilt
And thy Being mild
In torment and dismay
To death beguiled

Fafnir, I shall say then,
Thou art better dead
For the knights have burnt thy grass
And thou couldst not have fed.

The Airy Christ

(After reading Dr Rieu's translation of St Mark's Gospel)

Who is this that comes in grandeur, coming from the
     blazing East?
This is he we had not thought of, this is he the airy Christ.

Airy, in an airy manner in an airy parkland walking,
Others take him by the hand, lead him, do the talking.

But the Form, the airy One, frowns an airy frown,
What they say he knows must be, but he looks aloofly down,

Looks aloofly at his feet, looks aloofly at his hands,
Knows they must, as prophets say, nailèd be to wooden bands.

As he knows the words he sings, that he sings so happily
Must be changed to working laws, yet sings he ceaselessly.

Those who truly hear the voice, the words, the happy song,
Never shall need working laws to keep from doing wrong.

Deaf men will pretend sometimes they hear the song, the words,
And make excuse to sin extremely; this will be absurd.

Heed it not. Whatever foolish men may do the song is cried
For those who hear, and the sweet singer does not care that he
    was crucified.

For he does not wish that men should love him more than
    anything
Because he died; he only wishes they would hear him sing.

Loin de l'Etre

You don't look at all well, quite loin de l'être in fact,
Poor pale-face what's the matter, dont they know?
Oh they dont know, but still I dont feel well
Nor ever shall, my name is *Loin de l'Etre.*

They stood on the empty terrace above the precipice
When this conversation took place
Between the affectionate but exasperated friend
And the invalid.   It is not possible to be
Ill and merry, poor *Loin de l'Etre* sighed
And forced a smile, but oh she was so tired.
So tired, called Echo, so tired.

Now pull yourself together, cried the friend,
Together, cried Echo,
I must leave you now for a tick, she said,
Mind you dont get edgy looking at the precipice.
The lovely invalid sighed, Loin de l'être,
And Echo taking the form of a handsome young man
Cried, *Loin de l'Etre* and took her away with him.

The Singing Cat

I T was a little captive cat
    Upon a crowded train
His mistress takes him from his box
    To ease his fretful pain.

She holds him tight upon her knee
    The graceful animal
And all the people look at him
    He is so beautiful.

But oh he pricks and oh he prods
    And turns upon her knee
Then lifteth up his innocent voice
    In plaintive melody.

He lifteth up his innocent voice
    He lifteth up, he singeth
And to each human countenance
    A smile of grace he bringeth.

He lifteth up his innocent paw
    Upon her breast he clingeth
And everybody cries, Behold
    The cat, the cat that singeth.

He lifteth up his innocent voice
    He lifteth up, he singeth
And all the people warm themselves
    In the love his beauty bringeth.

The Jungle Husband

Dearest Evelyn, I often think of you
  Out with the guns in the jungle stew
Yesterday I hittapotamus
I put the measurements down for you but they got lost in
    the fuss
It's not a good thing to drink out here
You know, I've practically given it up dear.
Tomorrow I am going alone a long way
Into the jungle. It is all grey
But green on top
Only sometimes when a tree has fallen
The sun comes down plop, it is quite appalling.
You never want to go in a jungle pool
In the hot sun, it would be the act of a fool
Because it's always full of anacondas, Evelyn, not looking
    ill-fed
I'll say. So no more now, from your loving husband,
    Wilfred.

Longing for Death because of Feebleness

OH would that I were a reliable spirit careering around
Congenially employed and no longer by *feebleness* bound
Oh who would not leave the flesh to become a reliable spirit
Possibly travelling far and acquiring merit.

The Starling

I will never leave you darling
To be eaten by the starling
For I love you more than ever
In the wet and stormy weather

Thus to the husband sang the wife
That loved him more than his own life
Oh at these words the husband felt
Each hair rise separate upon his icy pelt.

He let himself down from out his room
He went upon the ancient mountain
And there he quite forgot his gloom
As he trod the torrent's icy fountain.

Cold, cold, icy cold,
Cold, cold, cold I am,
Cold has no place in my wife's warm thought
There she will have me cradled and wraught.
Oh nothing, nothing, nothing I
He cried, that in her thinking does not lie.

Then he doffed his clothes and quickly froze
In the ice of the ancient mountain-side
And there in an icy happy doze
He doth for evermore abide.

Down in the valley waits the wife
That loved him more than his own life
And still she sings, in hope to lure
Him to her side again, Be very sure

I will never leave you darling
To be eaten by the starling
For I love you more than ever
In the wet and stormy weather.

I Remember

IT was my bridal night I remember,
An old man of seventy-three
I lay with my young bride in my arms,
A girl with t.b.
It was wartime, and overhead
The Germans were making a particularly heavy raid on
Hampstead.
What rendered the confusion worse, perversely
Our bombers had chosen that moment to set out for Germany.
Harry, do they ever collide?
I do not think it has ever happened,
Oh my bride, my bride.

Songe d'Athalie

(from Racine)

IT was a dream and shouldn't I bother about a dream?
But it goes on you know, tears me rather.
Of course I try to forget it but it will not let me.
Well it was on an extraordinarily dark night at midnight
My mother Queen Jezebel appeared suddenly before me
Looking just as she did the day she died, dressed grandly.
It was her pride you noticed, nothing she had gone through
    touched that
And she still had the look of being most carefully made up
She always made up a lot she didn't want people to know
    how old she was

She spoke: Be warned my daughter, true girl to me, she said,
Do not suppose the cruel God of the Jews has finished with you,
I am come to weep your falling into his hands, my child.
With these appalling words my mother,
This ghost, leant over me stretching out her hands
And I stretched out my hands too to touch her
But what was it, oh this is horrible, what did I touch?
Nothing but the mangled flesh and the breaking bones
Of a body that the dogs tearing quarrelled over.

Why are the Clergy . . . ?

WHY are the clergy of the Church of England
    Always altering the words of the prayers in the Prayer
    Book?
Cranmer's touch was surer than theirs, do they not respect
    him?
For instance last night in church I heard
(I italicise the interpolation)
'The Lord bless you and keep you *and all who are dear unto*
    you'
As the blessing is a congregational blessing and meant to be
This is questionable on theological grounds
But is it not offensive to the ear and also ludicrous?
That 'unto' is a particularly ripe piece of idiocy
Oh how offensive it is. I suppose we shall have next
'Lighten our darkness we beseech thee oh Lord *and the*
    darkness of all who are dear unto us.'
It seems a pity. Does Charity object to the objection?
Then I cry, and not for the first time to that smooth face
Charity, have pity.

The Fairy Bell

A renegade poet, having taken to journalism for more money, is rebuked by his Muse in the form of an old gentleman; he cuts her throat.

A DISMAL bell hung in the belfry
And clanged a dismal tune
And back and forth the bats did fly
Wherever there was room.

He seemed a melancholy but a reasonable creature,
Yet I could see about his hat as it were this belfry steeple.

The agony through which I go,
He said, is something that you ought to know
And something that you will know too
When I have finished telling you.

He took my hand, I could not choose but stand,
Perhaps for his own sake he should not have done this?
Yet I thought Death was the best prize, if he won this.

Oh, the sad music of the backward and forth
Flying of the bats, pleading for worth,
But in this perhaps again I was wrong—
That there was for him some enjoyment in their song?

It is done now and I cannot trouble to rue it,
I took his gullet in my hand and with my knife cut through it.

But still in my head I sometimes hear the soft tune
Of the belfry bats moaning to find more room
And the ding-dong of that imaginary sound
Is as grateful as a fairy bell tolling by waters drowned.

Childe Rolandine

Dark was the day for Childe Rolandine the artist
When she went to work as a secretary-typist
And as she worked she sang this song
Against oppression and the rule of wrong:

It is the privilege of the rich
To waste the time of the poor
To water with tears in secret
A tree that grows in secret
That bears fruit in secret
That ripened falls to the ground in secret
And manures the parent tree
Oh the wicked tree of hatred and the secret
The sap rising and the tears falling.

Likely also, sang the Childe, my soul will fry in hell
Because of this hatred, while in heaven my employer does well
And why should he not, exacerbating though he be but
        generous
Is it his fault I must work at a work that is tedious?
Oh heaven sweet heaven keep my thoughts in their night den
Do not let them by day be spoken.

But then she sang, Ah why not? tell all, speak, speak,
Silence is vanity, speak for the whole truth's sake.

And rising she took the bugle and put it to her lips, crying:
There is a Spirit feeds on our tears, I give him mine,
Mighty human feelings are his food
Passion and grief and joy his flesh and blood
That he may live and grow fat we daily die
This cropping One is our immortality.

Childe Rolandine bowed her head and in the evening
Drew the picture of the spirit from heaven.

Parents

Parents who barely can afford it
  Should not send their children to public schools ill will
    reward it
That skimping and saving and giving up
That seems so unselfish will buy you a pup
Oh what an ugly biting bow-wow
Well Colonel, how does it go now?
Your son aged twenty-two wears a glittering blazer
His conversation about ponds and ducks, oh happy fool,
Is interrupted to speak of his school
As if at fault he'd allowed
Momentarily that pond to draw him from being proud.
Ah, so hardly won through to it, Colonel,
Is to attach too much importance to it
But he's saved; ponds, duck, fish in dark water
Have a tight hold of him.   It is your daughter
Colonel, who is wholly corrupted.
Women when they are snobbish do not loaf
Look at fish, are not oafish
But are persistently mercenary, cold, scheming and calculating,
This in a young girl is revolting.
Oh beautiful brave mother, the wife of the colonel,
How could you allow your young daughter to become aware
    of the scheming?
If you had not, it might have stayed a mere dreaming
Of palaces and princes, girlish at worst.
Oh to become sensible about social advance at seventeen is
    to be lost.

The Queen and the Young Princess

MOTHER, Mother, let me go
There are so many things I wish to do
My child, the time is not yet ripe
You are not yet ready for life
But what is my life that is to come to be?
Much the same, child, as it has been for me
But Mother you often say you have a headache
Because of the crown you wear for duty's sake
So it is, so it is, a headache I have
And that is what you must grow up to carry to the grave.
But in between Mother do you not enjoy the pleasant weather
And to see the bluebottle and the soft feather?
Ah my child, that joy you speak of must be a pleasure
Of human stature, not the measure
Of animals', who have no glorious duty
To perform, no headache and so cannot see beauty
Up, child, up, embrace the headache and the crown
Marred pleasure's best, shadow makes the sun strong.

Harold's Leap

Harold, are you asleep?
Harold, I remember your leap,
It may have killed you
But it was a brave thing to do.
Two promontories ran high into the sky,
He leapt from one rock to the other
And fell to the sea's smother.
Harold was always afraid to climb high,
But something urged him on,
He felt he should try.
I would not say that he was wrong,
Although he succeeded in doing nothing but die.
Would you?
Ever after that steep
Place was called Harold's Leap.
It was a brave thing to do.

Behind the Knight

BEHIND the Knight sits hooded Care
And as he rides she speaks him fair,
She lays her hand in his sable muff,
Ride he never so fast he'll not cast her off.

My Cats

I LIKE to toss him up and down
A heavy cat weighs half a Crown
With a hey do diddle my cat Brown.

I like to pinch him on the sly
When nobody is passing by
With a hey do diddle my cat Fry.

I like to ruffle up his pride
And watch him skip and turn aside
With a hey do diddle my cat Hyde.

Hey Brown and Fry and Hyde my cats
That sit on tombstones for your mats.

"Oh stubborn race of Cadmus' seed..."

IT is the bird of burial
I invoke for my brother's funeral
I throw the dust in Creon's eyes
Not my father is blind but my uncle is
And when they have killed me I will stand in the dark hall
And cry: Orcus, see that my sister does not suffer at all.

The Ambassador

'... known also among the Phoenicians as Casmilus' (Lempriere.)

UNDERNEATH the broad hat is the face of the Ambassador
    He rides on a white horse through hell looking two ways.
Doors open before him and shut when he has passed.
He is master of the mysteries and in the market place
He is known.   He stole the trident, the girdle,
The sword, the sceptre and many mechanical instruments.
Thieves honour him.   In the underworld he rides carelessly.
Sometimes he rises into the air and flies silently.

Thought is Superior

THOUGHT is superior to dress and circumstance,
    It is thought proud thought that sets the world in a
    dance.
And what is the greatest thought since the world begun?
Copernicus's discovery that the earth goes round the sun.

The Deserter

THE world is come upon me, I used to keep it a long way
off,
But now I have been run over and I am in the hands of the
hospital staff.
They say as a matter of fact I have not been run over it's
imagination,
But they all agree I should be kept in bed under observation.
I must say it's very comfortable here, nursie has such nice
hands,
And every morning the doctor comes and lances my
tuberculous glands.
He says he does nothing of the sort, but I have my own
feelings about that,
And what they are if you don't mind I shall continue to keep
under my hat.
My friend, if you call it a friend, has left me; he says I am
a deserter to ill health,
And that the things I should think about have made off for
ever, and so has my wealth.
Portentous ass, what to do about him's no strain
I shall quite simply never speak to the fellow again.

The After-thought

RAPUNZEL Rapunzel let down your hair
It is I your beautiful lover who am here
And when I come up this time I will bring a rope ladder
    with me
And then we can both escape into the dark wood immediately.
This must be one of those things, as Edgar Allan Poe says
    somewhere in a book,
Just because it is perfectly obvious one is certain to overlook.
I wonder sometimes by the way if Poe isn't a bit introspective,
One can stand about getting rather reflective,
But thinking about the way the mind works, you know,
Makes one inactive, one simply doesn't know which way to go;
Like the centipede in the poem who was corrupted by the toad
And ever after never did anything but lie in the middle of the
    road,
Or the old gurus of India I've seen, believe it or not,
Standing seventy-five years on their toes until they dropped.
Or Titurel, for that matter, in his odd doom
Crying: I rejoice because by the mercy of the Saviour I
    continue to live in the tomb.
What's that darling? You cant' hear me?
That's odd. I can hear you quite distinctly.

The Warden

(To the tune of: 'They played in the beautiful garden . . .')

THEY played in the beautiful garden
   Those children of high degree,
But she sighed as she swam with the Warden
In the depths of the Zuyder Zee.

Oh why did you take me away
From the children I loved so well?
I had other plans in my heart, dear
For the child of my latest spell.

The Warden has decked her with seaweed,
And shells of an ancient design,
But she sighs as she presses his fingers,
My heart can never be thine.

He sits in the golden chair
With the child he would call his own,
But the beautiful child has expired,
He nurses a sea-green stone.

Le Singe Qui Swing

(*to the tune of Green-sleeves*)

OUTSIDE the house
The swinging ape
Swung to and fro,
Swung to and fro,
And when midnight shone so clear
He was still swinging there.

Oh ho the swinging ape,
The happy peaceful animal,
Oh ho the swinging ape,
I love to see him gambol.

The Weak Monk

THE monk sat in his den,
He took the mighty pen
And wrote "Of God and Men."

One day the thought struck him
It was not according to Catholic doctrine;
His blood ran dim.

He wrote till he was ninety years old,
Then he shut the book with a clasp of gold
And buried it under the sheep fold.

He'd enjoyed it so much, he loved to plod,
And he thought he'd a right to expect that God
Would rescue his book alive from the sod.

Of course it rotted in the snow and rain;
No one will ever know now what he wrote of God and men.
For this the monk is to blame.

The Roman Road

A Christian speaks to a Lion in the Arena

OH Lion in a peculiar guise,
  Sharp Roman road to Paradise,
Come eat me up, I'll pay thy toll
With all my flesh, and keep my soul.

The Death Sentence

COLD as No Plea,
  Yet wild with all negation,
Weeping I come
To my heart's destination,
To my last bed
Between th' unhallowed boards—
The Law allows it
And the Court awards.

Le Majeur Ydow

'EH bien! Marche!', fit le Majeur Ydow,
  'Any more gentlemen like that? *I'll see them off!'*

But there were no gentlemen really, only the phantoms
He warred with in his perpetual tantrums.

Cool and Plain

COOL and plain
   Cool and plain
Was the message of love on the windowpane.
Soft and quiet
Soft and quiet
It vanished away in the fogs of night.

The Conventionalist

FOURTEEN-YEAR-OLD, why must you giggle and dote,
   Fourteen-year-old, why are you such a goat?
I'm fourteen years old, that is the reason,
I giggle and dote in season.

Pad, Pad

I ALWAYS remember your beautiful flowers
And the beautiful kimono you wore
When you sat on the couch
With that tigerish crouch
And told me you loved me no more.

What I cannot remember is how I felt when you were unkind
All I know is, if you were unkind now I should not mind.
Ah me, the capacity to feel angry, exaggerated and sad
The years have taken from me.   Softly I go now, pad pad.

The River God

(OF THE RIVER MIMRAM IN HERTFORDSHIRE)

I MAY be smelly and I may be old,
Rough in my pebbles, reedy in my pools,
But where my fish float by I bless their swimming
And I like the people to bathe in me, especially women.
But I can drown the fools
Who bathe too close to the weir, contrary to rules.
And they take a long time drowning
As I throw them up now and then in a spirit of clowning.
Hi yih, yippity-yap, merrily I flow,
O I may be an old foul river but I have plenty of go.
Once there was a lady who was too bold
She bathed in me by the tall black cliff where the water
     runs cold,
So I brought her down here
To be my beautiful dear.
Oh will she stay with me will she stay
This beautiful lady, or will she go away?
She lies in my beautiful deep river bed with many a weed
To hold her, and many a waving reed.
Oh who would guess what a beautiful white face lies there
Waiting for me to smoothe and wash away the fear
She looks at me with.   Hi yih, do not let her
Go.   There is no one on earth who does not forget her
Now.   They say I am a foolish old smelly river
But they do not know of my wide original bed
Where the lady waits, with her golden sleepy head.
If she wishes to go I will not forgive her.

The Wanderer

'TWAS the voice of the Wanderer, I heard her exclaim,
   You have weaned me too soon, you must nurse me again,
She taps as she passes at each window pane,
Pray, does she not know that she taps in vain?

Her voice flies away on the midnight wind,
But would she be happier if she were within?
She is happier far where the night winds fall,
And there are no doors and no windows at all.

No man has seen her, this pitiful ghost,
And no woman either, but heard her at most,
Sighing and tapping and sighing again,
You have weaned me too soon, you must nurse me again.

The Orphan Reformed

THE orphan is looking for parents
  She roams the world over
Looking for parents and cover.
She looks at this pair and that
Cries, Father, Mother,
Likes these, does not like those,
Stays for a time; goes,
Crying, Oh hearts of stone.
But really she is better alone.
Orphan, the people who will not be your parents are not evil,
Not the devil.
But still she cries, Father, Mother
Must I be alone for ever?
Yes you must. Oh wicked orphan, oh rebellion,
Must an orphan not be alone is that your opinion?
At last the orphan is reformed. Now quite
Alone she goes; now she is right.
Now when she cries, Father, Mother, it is only to please.
Now the people do not mind, now they say she is a mild tease.

O QUEEN of Heaven
　　Have pity on me,
My heart is bared
For you to see.

Forgive, forgive
The heart that lies
In anguish bared
Before your eyes.

Mother of God
Behold my heart,
Its sin and stain,
Its bitter smart;

In pity turn
Your pitying gaze
Upon my heart,
And its hopes raze

Quite to the ground,
For there are yet
Some hopes that are
Too highly set.

O lop each hope
And lay it low,
And quench the fire
Of my heart's glow.

For still I hope
He may return,
And while I hope,
Still must I burn

All with desire
That waits on hope
As doth the hangman
On the rope.

Hope and desire,
All unfulfilled,
Have more than rope
And hangman killed.

If I lie down

I F I lie down on my bed I must be here,
But if I lie down in my grave I may be elsewhere.

Girls !

GIRLS! although I am a woman
I always try to appear human

Unlike Miss So-and-So whose greatest pride
Is to remain always in the VI Form and not let down
    the side

Do not sell the pass dear, don't let down the side,
That is what this woman said and a lot of balsy stuff
    beside
(Oh the awful balsy nonsense that this woman cried.)

Girls!   I will let down the side if I get a chance
And I will sell the pass for a couple of pence.

Autumn

HE told his life story to Mrs. Courtly
    Who was a widow. 'Let us get married shortly',
He said. 'I am no longer passionate,
But we can have some conversation before it is too late.'

Conviction (1)

CHRIST died for God and me
Upon the crucifixion tree
For God a spoken Word
For me a Sword
For God a hymn of praise
For me eternal days
For God an explanation
For me salvation.

Conviction (2)

I WALKED abroad in Easter Park,
I heard the wild dog's distant bark,
I knew my Lord was risen again,—
Wild dog, wild dog, you bark in vain.

Conviction (3)

THE shadow was so black,
I thought it was a cat,
But once in to it
I knew it
No more black
Than a shadow's back.

Illusion is a freak
Of mind;
The cat's to seek.

The Face

THERE is a face I know too well,
   A face I dread to see,
So vain it is, so eloquent
Of all futility.

It is a human face that hides
A monkey soul within,
That bangs about, that beats a gong,
That makes a horrid din.

Sometimes the monkey soul will sprawl
Athwart the human eyes,
And peering forth, will flesh its pads,
And utter social lies.

So wretched is this face, so vain,
So empty and forlorn,
You well may say that better far
This face had not been born.

Advice to Young Children

'CHILDREN who paddle where the ocean bed shelves
    steeply
Must take great care they do not,
Paddle too deeply.'

Thus spake the awful aging couple
Whose heart the years had turned to rubble.

But the little children, to save any bother,
Let it in at one ear and out at the other.

Edmonton, thy cemetery . . .

EDMONTON, thy cemetery
  In which I love to tread
Has roused in me a dreary thought
For all the countless dead,
Ah me, the countless dead.

Yet I believe that one is one
And shall for ever be,
And while I hold to this belief
I walk, oh cemetery,
Thy footpaths happily.

And I believe that two and two
Are but an earthly sum
Whose totalling has no part at all
In heavenly kingdom-come,
I love the dead, I cry, I love
Each happy happy one.

Till Doubt returns with dreary face
And fills my heart with dread
For all the tens and tens and tens
That must make up a hundred,
And I begin to sing with him
As if Belief had never been
Ah me, the countless dead, ah me
The countless countless dead.

The Governess

THE milky love of this bland child
  Her governess has quite beguiled,
And now they spend the hours talking,
Sometimes winding wool and sometimes walking.

Ah, will the Saviour . . . ?

THE cross begot me on the stone,
    My heart emits no further moan,
But fortified by funeral thought
Awaits the doom of the distraught.

Ah! will the Saviour never come
To unlock me from the tomb,
To requite the tears that falter
For a birth I could not alter?

The Virtuoso

THE portrait of my mother,
  In plaster lightly scored,
Has always protected me
From anything untoward;
In Manchester or Italy,
Wherever I have toured,
Upon its plinth
It beholds the zenith
Of my success on the pianoforte;
I ask no further reward,
I ask no further reward.

The Heavenly City

I SIGH for the heavenly country,
Where the heavenly people pass,
And the sea is as quiet as a mirror
Of beautiful beautiful glass.

I walk in the heavenly field,
With lilies and poppies bright,
I am dressed in a heavenly coat
Of polished white.

When I walk in the heavenly parkland
My feet on the pasture are bare,
Tall waves the grass, but no harmful
Creature is there.

At night I fly over the housetops,
And stand on the bright moony beams;
Gold are all heaven's rivers,
And silver her streams.

Love Me!

Love me, Love me, I cried to the rocks and the trees,
And Love me, they cried again, but it was only to tease.
Once I cried Love me to the people, but they fled like a
    dream,
And when I cried Love me to my friend, she began to scream.
Oh why do they leave me, the beautiful people, and only the
    rocks remain,
To cry Love me, as I cry Love me, and Love me again.

On the rock a baked sea-serpent lies,
And his eyelids close tightly over his violent eyes,
And I fear that his eyes will open and confound me with a
    mirthless word,
That the rocks will harp on for ever, and my Love me never
    be heard.

Dirge

From a friend's friend I taste friendship,
From a friend's friend love,
My spirit in confusion,
Long years I strove,
But now I know that never
Nearer I shall move,
Than a friend's friend to friendship,
To love than a friend's love.

Into the dark night
Resignedly I go,
I am not so afraid of the dark night
As the friends I do not know,
I do not fear the night above
As I fear the friends below.

Study to Deserve Death

STUDY to deserve Death, they only may
Who fought well upon their earthly day,
Who never sheathed their swords or ran away.

See, such a man as this now proudly stands,
Pale in the clasp of Death, and to his hands
Yields up the sword, but keeps the laurel bands

Honour and emulate his warrior soul,
For whom the sonorous death-bells toll;
He after journeying has reached his goal.

Prate not to me of suicide,
Faint heart in battle, not for pride
I say Endure, but that such end denied
Makes welcomer yet the death that's to be died.

Lady 'Rogue' Singleton

Come, wed me, Lady Singleton,
And we will have a baby soon
And we will live in Edmonton
Where all the friendly people run.

I could never make you happy darling,
Or give you the baby you want,
I would always very much rather, dear,
Live in a tent.

I am not a cold woman, Henry,
But I do not feel for you,
What I feel for the elephants and the miasmas
And the general view.

The Broken Heart

('Oh, Sing to me Gypsy')

HE told me he loved me,
He gave me red roses,
Twelve crimson roses
As red as my blood.

The roses he gave me,
The roses are withered,
Twelve crimson roses
As red as my blood.

The roses are withered,
But here on my breast, far
Redder than they is
The red of my heart's blood.

He told me he loved me,
He gave me red roses,
Twelve crimson roses
As red as my blood.

The Repentance of Lady T

I LOOK in the glass
  Whose face do I see?
It is the face
Of Lady T.

I wish to change,
How can that be?
Oh Lamb of God
Change me, change me.

Happiness

HAPPINESS is silent, or speaks equivocally for friends,
Grief is explicit and her song never ends,
Happiness is like England, and will not state a case,
Grief like Guilt rushes in and talks apace.

The Magic Morning

THE boating party
  Started at dawn from Clarté.
Lightly lightly they stepped into the green boat
(The Lady Marion has left behind her golden coat).
Marion d'Arcy and Charley Dake
Were the only ones. He rowed her upon the lake.
He rowed her across the lake until the green shallows
Paled in a waxen lily litter striped with swallows.
And now the morning sun flecks the dark trees
And lightly the mauve sedge moves in a little breeze.

Charley Dake loves the ducal girl
But her eyelids flick flick upon his thoughts' whirl.
Oh my ducal girl, cries Charley in a fit
Of love-spasm. He is Cupid-hit.
But the Lady Marion smiles and smiles
And so they go again upon the watery miles.

'Oh Charley, Charley, do not go upon the water'
Cries a friendly swan, 'with the Duke's daughter.
You wish to marry er, my boy-carrier? you can not support er
Oh do not go with the Duke's daughter.'

There is an island in the lake, old brick walled,
Where the laurestina climbs and is not spoiled.
What man will spoil the brick walls of their yellow brim?
Such a one as is nervy bold and grim.
(Such a one, says the swan, as has something in store for him.)

Flick flick the eyelids of the lady mark
Where a dark angel floats across her father's park.
All the green grass shivers in a warning,
Flee, Charley, flee the magic morning.

But Charley is folly-blind to the visitation
Of the dark angel of consternation.
Boldly he plucks a golden cup
Throws it in Marion's lap and does not look up.

Ah then the thunder peals and the waters bound
For who took the flower, the angel says, must be drowned.
So up rears the lake water and drags him underneath
Where in suffering he draws his last breath.
'Never more', cries the swan, 'shall Charley be seen,
He is underneath the waters of the mise-en-scène'.
(And 'Charley, Charley, Charley' cry the swan-instructed
        curlews
Ever after as they fly to their nests in the purlieus.)

But the ducal girl comes safe to land and takes her coat,
And goes off in the likeness of a slim stoat.

My Heart was Full

My heart was full of softening showers,
I used to swing like this for hours,
I did not care for war or death,
I was glad to draw my breath.

Croft

Aloft,
In the loft,
Sits Croft;
He is soft.

The Pleasures of Friendship

THE pleasures of friendship are exquisite,
  How pleasant to go to a friend on a visit!
I go to my friend, we walk on the grass,
And the hours and moments like minutes pass.

'Après la Politique, la Haine des Bourbons'

COUNT Flanders
Was eaten up with pride;
His dog Sanders
Thought only of his inside.

They were a precious couple,
And let the people feed on straw and rubble.

Bitter was the weather,
Bitter the people,
When they flung Count Flanders
From the church steeple.
Bitter was the weather,
Iron the ground,
When Dog Sanders died of a stomach wound.

Lot's Wife

'In that rich, oil-bearing region, it is probable that Lot's wife was turned into a pillar of asphalt—not salt.' (Sir William Whitebait, Member of the Institute of Mining Engineers.)

I LONG for the desolate valleys,
  Where the rivers of asphalt flow,
For here in the streets of the living,
Where my footsteps run to and fro,
Though my smile be never so friendly,
I offend wherever I go.

Yes, here in the land of the living,
Though a marriage be fairly sprung,
And the heart be loving and giving,
In the end it is sure to go wrong.

Then take me to the valley of asphalt,
And turn me to a river of stone,
That no tree may shift to my sighing,
Or breezes convey my moan.

Old Ghosts

'By one half as much power as the Roman Centurion.'
(de Quincey.)

I CAN call up old ghosts, and they will come,
But my art limps,—I cannot send them home.

Satin-Clad

SATIN-CLAD, with many a pearl,
Is this rich and wretched girl.
Does she weep? Her tears are crystal,
And she counts them as they fall.

Unpopular, lonely and loving

UNPOPULAR, lonely and loving,
  Elinor need not trouble,
For if she were not so loving,
She would not be so miserable.

Hast Du Dich Verirrt?

MY child, my child, watch how he goes,
  The man in Party coloured clothes.

Voices against England in the Night

'ENGLAND, you had better go,
There is nothing else that you ought to do,
You lump of survival value, you are too slow.

'England, you have been here too long,
And the songs you sing are the songs you sung
On a braver day.   Now they are wrong.

'And as you sing the sliver slips from your lips,
And the governing garment sits ridiculously on your hips.
It is a pity that you are still too cunning to make slips.'

Dr. Goebbels, that is the point,
You are a few years too soon with your jaunt,
Time and the moment is not yet England's daunt.

Yes, dreaming Germany, with your Urge and Night,
You must go down before English and American might.
It is well, it is well, cries the peace kite.

Perhaps England our darling will recover her lost thought
We must think sensibly about our victory and not be
distraught,
Perhaps America will have an idea, and perhaps not.

But they cried: Could not England, once the world's best,
Put off her governing garment and be better dressed
In a shroud, a shroud?   O history turn thy pages fast!

One of Many

You are only one of many
    And of small account if any,
You think about yourself too much.
This touched the child with a quick touch
And worked his mind to such a pitch
He threw his fellows in a ditch.
This little child
That was so mild
Is grown too wild.

Murder in the first degree, cried Old Fury,
Recording the verdict of the jury.

Now they are come to the execution tree.
The gallows stand wide.   Ah me, ah me.

Christ died for sinners, exclaimed the Prison Chaplain
        from his miscellany.
Weeping bitterly the little child cries: I die one of
        many.

'Ceci est digne de gens sans Dieu'
(Allen)

These hands so well articulated
    By brother's life-blood are contaminated
And still he walks, and still the shadows fall,
He clasps them.   There is nothing there at all.

When the Sparrow Flies

WHEN the sparrow flies to the delicate branch
  He seems to be a heavy one alighting there,
It is March, and the fine twigs dance
As the boisterous sparrow plunges masterfully.
Fly again to my heart oh my beloved,
My heart flies too high when you are absent.

Infelice

Walking swiftly with a dreadful duchess,
     He smiled too briefly, his face was as pale as sand,
He jumped into a taxi when he saw me coming,
Leaving me alone with a private meaning,
He loves me so much, my heart is singing.
Later at the Club when I rang him in the evening
They said: Sir Rat is dining, is dining, is dining,
No Madam, he left no message, ah how his silence speaks,
He loves me too much for words, my heart is singing.
The Pullman seats are here, the tickets for Paris, I am waiting,
Presently the telephone rings, it is his valet speaking,
Sir Rat is called away, to Scotland, his constituents,
(Ah the dreadful duchess, but he loves me best)
Best pleasure to the last, my heart is singing.
One night he came, it was four in the morning,
Walking slowly upstairs, he stands beside my bed,
Dear darling, lie beside me, it is too cold to stand speaking,
He lies down beside me, his face is like the sand,
He is in a sleep of love, my heart is singing.
Sleeping softly softly, in the morning I must wake him,
And waking he murmurs, I only came to sleep.
The words are so sweetly cruel, how deeply he must love me,
I say them to myself aloud, my heart is singing.
Now the sunshine strengthens, it is ten in the morning,
He is so timid in love, he only needs to know,
He is my little child, how can he come if I do not call him?
I will write and tell him everything, I take the pen and write:
I love you so much, my heart is singing.

Brickenden, Hertfordshire

SITTING alone of a summer's evening,
        I thought
Of the tragedy of unwatered country.
O little village of Brickenden,
Where is thy stream,
Translucent drain of thy manorial sward?
Thy sward is green,
Its source of verdancy guessed but unseen.
Where is thy stream?
I have beat every bound of this wild wood.
I have trod down its spiteful and detaining
        undergrowth,
Seeking a broad stream and contented fish,
Seeking but finding not.
Now that the sun
Sou'westering in the sky
Tells me that evening is come,
I rest
Oppressed
By thy wood's profligate viridity,
By thy wood's sap,
Child of a moisture that I cannot tap.

O woods of Brickenden, you have confounded me
By your appearance of humidity.
I see the pashy ground,
And round and round
My tired feet the rushes twine,
And frogs croak and the sweating slime
Is moved by an ambiguous brood
Of low and legless life.

Hadst thou thy stream,
O wood of Brickenden,
This had been
Paradise
But thy sap's virtue comes from dank earth's sweat,
And to be wet
Is not enough, O Wood.
Hadst thou thy stream,
O little village of Brickenden,
Thy stream
Had salined thee
By virtue of destinatory sea,
And thou hadst been
A Paradise.
But lacking stream
Art but a suppuration of earth's humours.
Sitting alone on a summer's evening,
I wept
For the tragedy of unwatered country.
Take thou my tears, O Brickenden,
They are thy rank sweat's sea.

The Failed Spirit

To those who are isolate
  War comes, promising respite,
Making what seems to be up to the moment the most
    successful endeavour
Against the fort of the failed spirit that is alone for ever.
Spurious failed spirit, adamantine wasture,
Crop, spirit, crop thy stony pasture!

The Boat

THE boat that took my love away
    He sent again to me
To tell me that he would not sleep
Alone beneath the sea.

The flower and fruit of love are mine
The ant, the fieldmouse and the mole,
But now a tiger prowls without
And claws upon my soul.

Love is not love that wounded bleeds
And bleeding sullies slow.
Come death within my hands and I
Unto my love will go.

Le Désert de l'Amour

I WANT to be your pinkie
I am tender to you
My heart opens like a cactus flower
Do you thinky I will do?

My heart is like a cactus
Not like a cactus flower
And I can kill love
Without entering her bower.

So they both thought.   But he was silent and she said:
I cannot see which way you are pointing, the sky is so dark red,
And when the sandstorm is over I will lie down on my bed.

Mother, among the Dustbins

MOTHER, among the dustbins and the manure
I feel the measure of my humanity, an allure
As of the presence of God.   I am sure

In the dustbins, in the manure, in the cat at play,
Is the presence of God, in a sure way
He moves there.   Mother, what do you say?

I too have felt the presence of God in the broom
I hold, in the cobwebs in the room,
But most of all in the silence of the tomb.

Ah! but that thought that informs the hope of our kind
Is but an empty thing, what lies behind?—
Naught but the vanity of a protesting mind

That would not die.   This is the thought that bounces
Within a conceited head and trounces
Inquiry.   Man is most frivolous when he pronounces.

Well Mother, I shall continue to think as I do,
And I think you would be wise to do so too,
Can you question the folly of man in the creation of God?
      Who are you?

The Deathly Child

THE deathly child is very gay,
He walks in the sunshine but no shadow falls his way,
He has come to warn us that one must go who would rather
stay.

Oh deathly child
With a heart of woe
And a smile on your face,
Who is it that must go?

He walks down the avenue, the trees
Have leaves that are silver where they are turned upon the
breeze.
He is more pale than the silver leaves more pale than these.

He walks delicately,
He has a delicate tread.
Why look, he leaves no mark at all
Where the dust is spread.

Over the café tables the talk is going to and fro,
And the people smile and they frown, but they do not know
That the deathly child walks.   Ah who is it that must go?

The Toll of the Roads

THE angels wept to see poor Tolly dead
He was a harmless simple creature without a thought in
his head.
Oh what is come upon him to make the road his death-bed?

Vater Unser

To the tune of the Londonderry Air

VATER unser,
　　Der Du im Himmel wohnst,
Behold thy child,
His prayers and his complaint.
He was conceived
In sin and born to set it on,
This sin is his,
His strength to act upon.
Oh, Father, heed
Thy child, let not the grave
Seal him in sin
Beyond thy power to save.
Strike at his strength,
Leave weakness only for her vaunt,
Vater Unser,
Du Der im Himmel wohnst.

The Lads of the Village

THE lads of the village, we read in the lay,
By medalled commanders are muddled away,
And the picture that the poet makes is not very gay.

Poet, let the red blood flow, it makes the pattern better,
And let the tears flow too, and grief stand that is their
    begetter,
And let man have his self-forged chain and hug every fetter.

For without the juxtaposition of muddles, medals and clay,
Would the picture be so very much more gay,
Would it not be a frivolous dance upon a summer's day?

Oh sigh no more: Away with the folly of commanders.
That will not take a better song upon the field of Flanders,
Or upon any field of experience where pain makes patterns
    the poet slanders.

Nourish Me on an Egg

NOURISH me on an egg, Nanny,
And ply with bottled stout,
And I'll grow to be a man
Before the secret's out.

Nourish me on an egg, Nanny,
With bottled stout to drink,
And I'll grow to be a man
Before you can think.

Nourish me on an egg, Nanny,
Don't wring your hands and weep,
Bring me a glass of stout
And close my eyes in sleep.

I do not Speak

I DO not ask for mercy for understanding for peace
And in these heavy days I do not ask for release
I do not ask that suffering shall cease

I do not pray to God to let me die
To give an ear attentive to my cry
To pause in his marching and not hurry by.

I do not ask for anything I do not speak
I do not question and I do not seek
I used to in the day when I was weak.

Now I am strong and lapped in sorrow
As in a coat of magic mail and borrow
From Time today and care not for tomorrow.

The Parklands

Through the Parklands, through the Parklands
Of the wild and misty north,
Walked a babe of seven summers
In a maze of infant wrath.

And I wondered and I murmured
And I stayed his restless pace
With a courteous eye I held him
In that unfrequented place.

Questioning I drew him to me
Touched him not but with an eye
Full of awful adult power
Challenged every infant sigh.

'Of what race and of what lineage',
Questioning I held him there,
'Art thou, boy?' He answered nothing
Only stood in icy stare.

Blue his eyes, his hair a flaxen
White fell gently on the breeze,
White his hair as straw and blue
His eyes as distant summer seas.

Steadfastly I gazed upon him
Gazed upon that infant face
Till the parted lips gave utterance
And he spake in measured pace:

'All abandoned are my father's
Parklands, and my mother's room
Houses but the subtle spider
Busy at her spinning loom.

'Dead my father, dead my mother,
Dead their son, their only child.'
'How is this when thou art living
Foolish boy, in wrath beguiled?'

'Ask me not,' he said, and moving
Passed into the distance dim.
High the sun stood in the heavens,
But no shadow followed him.

The Cousin

STANDING alone on a fence in a spasm,
I behold all life in a microcosm.
Behind me unknown with a beckoning finger
Is the house and well timbered park. I linger
Uncertain yet whether I should enter, take possession,
  still the nuisance
Of a huge ambition; and below me is the protesting
  face of my cousin.

'I'll have your heart'

I'LL have your heart, if not by gift my knife
Shall carve it out.   I'll have your heart, your life.

Flow, Flow, Flow

FLOW, flow, flow,
  Deep river running
To the sea.
Go, go, go,
Let all thy waters go
Over my head,
And when my bones are dead
Long may they lie
Upon the ocean bed,
Thy destiny.

Is it Wise?

Is it wise
To hug misery
To make a song of Melancholy
To weave a garland of sighs
To abandon hope wholly?
No, it is not wise.

Is it wise
To love Mortality
To make a song of Corruptibility
A chain of linked lies
To bind Mutability?
No, it is not wise.

Is it wise
To endure
To call up Old Fury
And Pain for a martyr's dowry
When Death's a prize
Easy to carry?
No, it is not wise.

Upon a Grave

To the tune 'Upon a bank in the greenwood as I lay'

UPON a grave
   In the churchyard as I lay,
An angel out of heaven
Came to me and he did say:
Your child is dead,
He singeth far away,
In Death is sorrow shed,
In Death is sorrow shed.

I raised my head
And mournfully I cried:
My son is dead
I was with him when he died.
He lies alone,
And worms his flesh divide.
In life is sorrow known,
In life is sorrow known.

The Fugitive's Ride

Across the bridge across the dyke
Foresworn by friend and foe alike,
I ride
The field upon the further side
Stretches before me and its wide
Horizon dark against dark sky
Beckons me on.   Dim homesteads lie
To left and right as I ride by.

It is a wet and steamy night,
More steamy night I have not seen
More steamy night there has not been,
I have rode on for many a mile
And now it does not rain
And has not done for quite a while
And all the plain
Lies limpid underneath the stars
That give an eerie light
And make the plain seem to be bright.
With standing water, deep or shallow?
Deep lake, or river?   Corn or fallow?
Lord, Lord, I cannot say
But warily I pick my way
This false starlight is worse than no light
To bewitch
The eyes and hide the gaping ditch.

What owl was that that howls upon
The trees athwart the stream
And have I been this way before
Or do I dream?

He seems to be a mournful one
That hoots to make a coward run
I hate to hear I hate to see
An owl that hoots so dismally
It makes my very blood run cold
No bird should dare to be so bold
I feel as fearful as he should
Who's done a dreadful deed of blood.

(Now hold up horse a moment pray,
Don't sidestep in that foolish way,
If you fall down upon the ground
There is a chance you will be drowned.)

A wetter plain I have not seen
A wetter plain there has not been
I say there has not been
A wetter plain
Since first I came
And may I die
If once again it does not rain.
In early dawn is this dark plain
Made darker still of darkness shorn
More dismaller but still the same
Lit by the ray that heralds day.

On, my poor horse, so lost so wan
That cannot understand
Why we must ride and ride and ride
And never yet come home
On you must go until you drop
For since time won't, I dare not stop.

Private Means is Dead

PRIVATE Means is dead
God rest his soul, officers and fellow-rankers said.

Captive Good, attending Captain Ill
Can tell us quite a lot about the Captain, if he will.

Major Portion
Is a disingenuous person
And as for Major Operation well I guess
We all know what his reputation is.

The crux and Colonel
Of the whole matter
(As you may read in the Journal
If it's not tattered)

Lies in the Generals Collapse, Debility, Panic and Uproar
Who are too old in any case to go to the War.

Bereavement

MARIA Holt
Was not the dolt
That people thought her.
Her face was full
Her mind not dull
She was my daughter.
She had so much to do so very much
And used to shuffle round upon a crutch,
The younger children always called her mother,
And so she was to sister and to brother
Poor wretch she's dead and now I am bereft
Of £60 a year to fill the place she left
I never paid a cent before; it is too bad,
It's worse to lose a lass than lose a lad.

Breughel

THE ages blaspheme
   The people are weak
As in a dream
They evilly speak.

Their words in a clatter
Of meaningless sound
Without form or matter
Echo around.

The people oh Lord
Are sinful and sad
Prenatally biassed
Grow worser born bad

They sicken oh Lord
They have no strength in them
Oh rouse up my God
And against their will win them.

Must thy lambs to the slaughter
Deliverèd be
With each son and daughter
Irrevocably?

From tower and steeple
Ring out funeral bells
Oh Lord save thy people
They have no help else.

Who Killed Lawless Lean?

T HE parrot
Is eating a carrot
In his cage in the garret

Why is the parrot's
Cage in the garret?
He is not a sage
Parrot: his words enrage.

Downstairs
In his bed
Lies the head
Of the family
He is dead.

And the brothers gather
Mutter utter would rather
Forget
The words the parrot
Said.

When high in his cage swinging
From the lofty ceiling
Sat the pet screaming:
'Who killed Lawless Lean?'
It was not at all fitting.

So they put the parrot
In his cage in the garret
And gave him a carrot
To keep him quiet.
He should be glad they did not wring his neck.

Portrait

SHE was not always so unkind I swear
And keep this thought that's all I have of her
Who was upon a time my only thought and care.

Sweet memory, hid from the light of truth
I'll keep thee, for I would not have thy worth
Questioned in Court of Law, nor answer for it on my oath,

But hid in my fond heart I'll carry thee
And to a fair false thought I'll marry thee
And when thy time is done I'll bury thee.

Now Pine-Needles

Now pine-needles
   You lie under the pine-trees
In the darkness of the pine-trees
The sun has not touched you
You are not brown because the sun has touched you
You are brown because you are dead.
The parent tree sighs in the wind
But it does not sigh for sadness
Only because the wind blows
The pine-tree sighs
Only because you are dead
You are brown.
Well, you do not know
That you were so and so
And are now so and so.
So why should I say
You were alive and are now dead
That your parent tree sighs in the wind?
I will sleep on you pine-needles,
Then I shall be
No more than the pine-tree
No more than the pine-tree's needles.

My Muse

MY Muse sits forlorn
    She wishes she had not been born
She sits in the cold
No word she says is ever told.

Why does my Muse only speak when she is unhappy?
She does not, I only listen when I am unhappy
When I am happy I live and despise writing
For my Muse this cannot but be dispiriting.

THE
Frog Prince

AND OTHER POEMS
WITH DRAWINGS BY THE AUTHOR

Stevie Smith

The Frog Prince

I AM a frog
I live under a spell
I live at the bottom
Of a green well

And here I must wait
Until a maiden places me
On her royal pillow
And kisses me
In her father's palace.

The story is familiar
Everybody knows it well
But do other enchanted people feel as nervous
As I do? The stories do not tell,

Ask if they will be happier
When the changes come
As already they are fairly happy
In a frog's doom?

I have been a frog now
For a hundred years
And in all this time
I have not shed many tears,

I am happy, I like the life,
Can swim for many a mile
(When I have hopped to the river)
And am for ever agile.

And the quietness,
Yes, I like to be quiet
I am habituated
To a quiet life,

But always when I think these thoughts
As I sit in my well
Another thought comes to me and says:
It is part of the spell

To be happy
To work up contentment
To make much of being a frog
To fear disenchantment

Says, It will be *heavenly*
To be set free,
Cries, *Heavenly* the girl who disenchants
And the royal times, *heavenly*,
And I think it will be.

Come, then, royal girl and royal times,
Come quickly,
I can be happy until you come
But I cannot be heavenly,
Only disenchanted people
Can be heavenly.

Tenuous and Precarious

TENUOUS and Precarious
Were my guardians,
Precarious and Tenuous,
Two Romans.

My father was Hazardous,
Hazardous,
Dear old man,
Three Romans.

There was my brother Spurious,
Spurious Posthumous,
Spurious was spurious
Was four Romans.

My husband was Perfidious,
He was perfidious,
Five Romans.

Surreptitious, our son,
Was surreptitious,
He was six Romans.

Our cat Tedious
Still lives,
Count not Tedious
Yet.

My name is Finis,
Finis, Finis,
I am Finis,
Six, five, four, three, two,
One Roman,
Finis.

A House of Mercy

It was a house of female habitation,
Two ladies fair inhabited the house,
And they were brave. For all though Fear knocked loud
Upon the door, and said he must come in,
They did not let him in.

There were also two feeble babes, two girls,
That Mrs. S. had by her husband had,
He soon left them and went away to sea,
Nor sent them money, nor came home again
Except to borrow back
Her Naval Officer's Wife's Allowance from Mrs. S.
Who gave it him at once, she thought she should.

There was also the ladies' aunt
And babes' great aunt, a Mrs. Martha Hearn Clode,
And she was elderly.
These ladies put their money all together
And so we lived.

I was the younger of the feeble babes
And when I was a child my mother died
And later Great Aunt Martha Hearn Clode died
And later still my sister went away.

Now I am old I tend my mother's sister
The noble aunt who so long tended us,
Faithful and True her name is. Tranquil.
Also Sardonic. And I tend the house.

It is a house of female habitation
A house expecting strength as it is strong
A house of aristocratic mould that looks apart
When tears fall; counts despair
Derisory. Yet it has kept us well. For all its faults,
If they are faults, of sternness and reserve,
It is a Being of warmth I think; at heart
A house of mercy.

The Best Beast of the Fat-Stock Show at Earls Court
(In monosyllables)

THE Best Beast of the Show
Is fat,
He goes by the lift—
They all do that.

This lift, large as a room,
(Yet the beasts bunch),
Goes up with a groan,
They have not oiled the winch.

Not yet to the lift
Goes the Best Beast,
He has to walk on the floor to make a show
First.

Great are his horns,
Long his fur,
The Beast came from the North
To walk here.

Is he not fat?
Is he not fit?
Now in a crown he walks
To the lift.

When he lay in his pen,
In the close heat,
His head lolled, his eyes
Were not shut for sleep.

Slam the lift door,
Push it up with a groan,
Will they kill the Beast now?
Where has he gone?

When he lay in the straw
His heart beat so fast
His sides heaved, I touched his side
As I walked past.

I touched his side,
I touched the root of his horns;
The breath of the Beast
Came in low moans.

Exeat

I REMEMBER the Roman Emperor, one of the cruellest of them,
Who used to visit for pleasure his poor prisoners cramped in
    dungeons,
So then they would beg him for death, and then he would say:
Oh no, oh no, we are not yet friends enough.
He meant they were not yet friends enough for him to give
    them death.
So I fancy my Muse says, when I wish to die:
Oh no, Oh no, we are not yet friends enough,

And Virtue also says:
We are not yet friends enough.

How can a poet commit suicide
When he is still not listening properly to his Muse,
Or a lover of Virtue when
He is always putting her off until tomorrow?

Yet a time may come when a poet or any person
Having a long life behind him, pleasure and sorrow,
But feeble now and expensive to his country
And on the point of no longer being able to make a decision
May fancy Life comes to him with love and says:
We are friends enough now for me to give you death;
Then he may commit suicide, then
He may go.

Easy

EASY in their ugly skins
Claudius and Gertrude were,
They liked as well as loving each other,
They were a humdrum pair.

Of all the people in that bloodstained play
They are the only ones
Who might have been living today.

Hamlet dimly perceived
They were not entirely of his times.
Their witless freedom of the ages
Irked him sometimes.

He, a man of two times—
His Yesterday, *his* Today—
Could not stretch
To their timelessness,
He was too much on edge.

Banausic, he called them, banausic,
A villainous banausic couple.
He turned to blow on his love for his father
And found it rubble.

Mouthing at Yesterday's ghostly manifestation
A sentence or two from Wittenberg, likely at least
To put a ghost in its place,
He discovered no satisfaction,
And no sense.

Sadly his heart heaved. Where was there a shield for him
Against banausic couples in their ugly skin
Easy, easy? There was never any ease for him.

Oh Christianity, Christianity

Oh Christianity, Christianity,
Why do you not answer our difficulties?
If He was God He was not like us,
He could not lose.

Can Perfection be less than perfection?
Can the creator of the Devil be bested by him?
What can the temptation to possess the earth have meant to
    Him
Who made and possessed it? What do you mean?

And Sin, how could He take our sins upon Him? What does
    it mean?
To take sin upon one is not the same
As to have sin inside one and feel guilty.

It is horrible to feel guilty,
We feel guilty because we are.
Was He horrible? Did He feel guilty?

You say He was born humble—but He was not,
He was born God—
Taking our nature upon Him. But then you say,
He was Perfect Man. Do you mean
Perfectly Man, meaning wholly; or Man without sin? Ah
Perfect Man without sin is not what we are.

Do you mean He did not know that He was God,
Did not know He was the Second Person of the Trinity?
(Oh, if He knew this, and was,
It was a source of strength for Him we do not have)
But this theology of 'emptying' you preach sometimes—
That He emptied Himself of knowing He was God—seems
A theology of false appearances
To mock your facts, as He was God, whether He knew He was
        or not.

Oh what do you mean, what do you mean?
You never answer our difficulties.

You say, Christianity, you say
That the Trinity is unchanging from eternity,
But then you say
At the incarnation He took
Our Manhood into the Godhead,
That did not have it before,
So it must have altered it,
Having it.

Oh what do you mean, what do you mean?
You never answer our questions.

Why do you rage?

WHY do you rage so much against Christ, against Him
Before Whom angel brightness grows dark, heaven dim?
Is He not wonderful, beautiful? Is He not Love?
Did He not come to call you from Heaven above?
Say, Yes; yes, He did; say, Yes; call Him this:
Truth, Beauty, Love, Wonder, Holiness.

Say, Yes. Do not always say, No.

Oh I would if I thought it were so,
Oh I know that you think it is so.

The True Tyrant
or
The Spirit of Duty Rebuked

OH my darling Goosey-Gander
Why do you always wish to wander
Evermore, evermore?

Now I have you safe at home
I will never let you roam
Ever more.

Then cried the lady from her kitchen
Standing in her chains of grass:
It is not Duty, it is Love
That will not let me pass
Evermore, evermore
Through the grass-enchainèd door, the grassy door.

'*Away, away!*'

Under Wrong Trees . . .
or
Freeing the Colonial Peoples

UNDER wrong trees
Walked the zombies

They were told to walk under oaks, you know,
But they preferred willows.

It was the first time they had been old
Enough not to do as they were told

They thus became
Not zombies
But *splendide*

Until one day they fell in
The river the willows were weeping in

Which was *stupide*
Of them, people said, and showed they were not old
Enough yet not to do as they were told.

But really I think this tale of wrong trees
Shows that they never were zombies

But men, women and men.

So why should we notice them?

I had a dream . . .

I HAD a dream I was Helen of Troy
In looks, age and circumstance,
But otherwise I was myself.

It was the ninth year of the siege
And I did not love anybody very much
Except perhaps Cassandra,
It was those peculiar eyes she had
As if she were short-sighted
That made me feel I could talk to her,
I would have loved anybody I could talk to.
I suppose you know how it's going to end, I said,
As well as I do? Dreams, dreams? They aren't dreams
You know. Do you know?

I used to walk on the walls
And look towards the Grecian tents . . .
It's odd, I said (to Cassandra, of course) how
Everything one has ever read about Troy
As they have always been such splendid writers who were
    writing
Naturally gets into one's conversation . . .
Where Cressid lay that night, except they did not say
How beastly Scamander looks under this sort of sky,
And the black Greek ships piled up on the seashore beyond
Like prison hulks, like slugs. So there we were
On the walls of Troy. But what I did not know,
And I could not get Cassandra to say either,
Was which of the Helen legends I was,
The phantom, with the real Helen in Egypt,
Or the flesh-and-blood one here
That Menelaus would take back to Sparta.

Remembering this, that there was still some uncertainty,
Raised my spirits. I must say
Dispiritedness was what we were all sunk in,
And though the Royal Family may have seemed spectral
Their dispiritedness was substantial enough, and I dare say
The Greeks were in much the same case, dispirited;
Well, nine years there had been of it, and now
The heavy weather, and the smells
From the battlefield, when the wind was in that direction,
And the spirit of the men, too, on both sides,
This was substantial enough; it seemed to me
Like the spirit of all armies, on all plains, in all wars, the
    men
No longer thinking why they were there
Or caring, but going on; like the song the English used to
    sing
In the first world war: We're here because, we're here
    because,
We're here because, we're here. This was the only time
I heard Cassandra laugh, when I sung this to her. I said:
There you are, you laugh; that shows you are not nearly so
Religious as you think. That's blasphemous, that laugh,
Sets you free. But then she got frightened. All right, I said,
Don't be free, go along and finish up on Clytemnestra's
    sword-point,
Pinked like a good girl. I used to get so cross.
Paris was stupid, it was impossible to talk to him.
Hector might have been different, at least he understood
    enough
To be offended—fear of the gods again, I suppose—because
When I said: Well, you know what the Trojan Women
Are going to say about the sack of Troy and being led away
Into captivity, they are going to say: If these things
Had not happened to us we should not be remembered. I
    hope that

Will be a comfort to you. He was angry and said
I should bring ill luck to Troy by my impiety, so I laughed
But I felt more like crying. I went into our palace then
And into my own room. But the heaviness of the sky
Still oppressed me, and the sad colours of rust and blood
I saw everywhere, as Cassandra saw too. Oh, I thought,
It is an ominous eternal moment I am captive in, it is always
This heavy weather, these colours, and the smell of the dead
    men.
It is curious to be caught in a moment of pause like this,
As a river pauses before it plunges in a great waterfall.
I was at home with these people at least in this, that we
    wished
It was over and done with. But oh, Cassandra, I said,
    catching hold of her,
For she was running away, I shall never make
That mischievous laughing Helen, who goes home with
    Menelaus
And over her needlework, in the quiet palace, laughs,
Telling her story, and cries: Oh shameful me. I am only at
    home
In this moment of pause, where feelings, colours and spirits
    are substantial,
But people are ghosts. When the pause finishes
I shall wake.

Dear Child of God

DEAR child of God
With the tears on your face
And your hands clasped in anger
What is the matter with your race?

In the beginning, Father,
You made the terms of our survival
That we should use our intelligence
To kill every rival.

The poison of this ferocity
Runs in our nature,
And O Lord thou knowest
How it nourishes thy creatures.

Oh what a lively poison it was
To bring us to full growth,
Is then becoming loving
As much as our life is worth?

It is a price I would pay
To grow loving and kind,
The price of my life
And the life of human kind.

Father in heaven
Dear Father of peacefulness
It is not often we remember
You put this poison in us,

Generally we stand
With the tears on our face
And our hands clasped in anger,
Faithful but unfortunate.

The Wedding Photograph

GOODBYE Harry I must have you by me for a time
But once in the jungle you must go off to a higher clime
The old lion on his slow toe
Will eat you up, that is the way you will go.

Oh how I shall like to be alone on the jungle path
But you are all right now for the photograph
So smile Harry smile and I will smile too
Thinking what is going to happen to you,
It is the death wish lights my beautiful eyes
But people think you are lucky to go off with such a pretty
    prize.

Ah feeble me that only wished alone to roam
Yet dared not without marrying leave home
Ah woe, burn fire, burn in eyes' sheathing
Fan bright fear, fan fire in Harry's breathing.

Phèdre

I WONDER why Proust should have thought
The lines from Racine's Phèdre
    Depuis que sur ces bords les dieux ont envoyé
    La fille de Minos et de Pasiphaé to be
Entirely devoid of meaning,
To me they seem
As lucid as they are alarming.

I wonder why
The actresses I have seen
Playing Phèdre
Always indulge
In such mature agonising.
Phèdre was young,
(This is as clear in Racine as Euripides)
She was young,
A girl caught in a trap, a girl
Under the enforcement
Of a goddess.
I dare say Phèdre
In fact I'm sure of it
Was by nature
As prim as Hippolytus,
Poor girl, poor girl, what could she do
But be ashamed and hang herself,
Poor girl.

How awful the French actress
Marie Bell
Made her appear.
Poor Phèdre,
Not only to be shamed by her own behaviour,
Enforced by that disgusting goddess,
Ancient enemy
Of her family,

But nowadays to have to be played
By actresses like Marie Bell
In awful ancient agonising, something painful.

Now if I
Had been writing this story
I should have arranged for Theseus
To die,
(Well, *he* was old)
And then I should have let
Phèdre and Hippolytus
Find Aricie out
In some small meanness,
Say
Eating up somebody else's chocolates,
Half a pound of them, soft centred.
Secretly in bed at night, alone,
One after another,
Positively wolfing them down.
This would have put Hip. off,
And Phaedra would be there too
And he would turn and see
That she was pretty disgusted, too,
So then they would have got married
And everything would have been respectable,
And the wretched Venus could have lumped it,
Lumped, I mean' Phèdre
Being the only respectable member
Of her awful family,
And being happy.

I should have liked one member
Of that awful family
To be happy,
What with Ariadne auf Naxos,
And Pasiphaé and that awful animal,
And Minos sitting judging the Dead
In those awful dark halls.
Yes, I should like poor honourable simple sweet prim Phèdre
To be happy. One would have to be pretty simple
To be happy with a prig like Hippolytus,
But she was simple.
I think it might have been a go,
If I were writing the story
I should have made it a go.

Everything Is Swimming

EVERYTHING is swimming in a wonderful wisdom
She said everything was swimming in a wonderful wisdom
Silly ass
What a silly woman
Perhaps she is drunk
No I think it is mescalin
Silly woman
What a silly woman
Yes perhaps it is mescalin
It must be something
Her father, they say . . .
And that funny man William . . .
Silly ass
What a silly woman

Elle continua de rire comme une hyène.

147

'The Persian'

THE gas fire
Seemed quite a friend
Such a funny little humming noise it made
And it had a name, too, carved on it you know,
'The Persian'. The Persian!
Ha ha ha; ha ha.

Now Agnes, pull yourself together.
You and your friends.

Emily writes such a good letter

MABEL was married last week
So now only Tom left

The doctor didn't like Arthur's cough
I have been in bed since Easter

A touch of the old trouble

I am downstairs today
As I write this
I can hear Arthur roaming overhead

He loves to roam
Thank heavens he has plenty of space to roam in

We have seven bedrooms
And an annexe

Which leaves a flat for the chauffeur and his wife

We have much to be thankful for

The new vicar came yesterday
People say he brings a breath of fresh air

He leaves me cold
I do not think he is a gentleman

Yes, I remember Maurice very well
Fancy getting married at his age
She must be a fool

You knew May had moved?
Since Edward died she has been much alone

It was cancer

No, I know nothing of Maud
I never wish to hear her name again
In my opinion Maud
Is an evil woman

Our char has left
And a good riddance too
Wages are very high in Tonbridge

Write and tell me how you are, dear,
And the girls,
Phoebe and Rose
They must be a great comfort to you
Phoebe and Rose.

November

In the dawn of a sumptuous November
I left my house in the park
I went for a walk in the park.

The mists had been grey and ephemeral
The mists they were damp and ephemeral
As they clung to the trees in the park
And swayed o'er the grass of the park,
They swayed o'er the grass of the park.

But the sun rose up red in a sumptuous glow
And made the mists rosy where'er they did blow
And all the great park in a rosiness lay
In that sumptuous dawn of a sumptuous day.

What made all spectacular, especially spectacular
Was the black of the trees as they stood, a particular
Blackness so damp, so bare and so dark,
As they stood 'gainst the sun in the sumptuous park,
As they stood 'gainst the sun in the park.

Monsieur Pussy-Cat, blackmailer

C'est un grand Monsieur Pussy-Cat
Who lives on the mat
Devant un feu énorme
And that is why he is so fat,
En effet il sait quelque chose
Et fait chanter son hôte,
Raison de plus pourquoi
He has such a glossy coat.
Ah ha, Monsieur Pussy-Cat
Si grand et si gras,
Take care you don't *pousser trop*
The one who gives you such *jolis plats.*

Si peu séduisante

Il était une petite fille de dix ans,
Si peu séduisante,
Qui entra dans le wagon-restaurant
Pour retrouver ses parents.
Elle portait son school uniform,
Si peu séduisante,
And a perfectly frightful little pair of shoes,
Mais ses yeux, malgré des lunettes hideuses,
Etaient si pleins de bonté et de franchise
Que tout autre aspect of this little schoolgirl,
Si peu séduisante,
Really only made one like her more.

To Carry the Child

To carry the child into adult life
Is good? I say it is not,
To carry the child into adult life
Is to be handicapped.

The child in adult life is defenceless
And if he is grown-up, knows it,
And the grown-up looks at the childish part
And despises it.

The child, too, despises the clever grown-up,
The man-of-the-world, the frozen,
For the child has the tears alive on his cheek
And the man has none of them.

As the child has colours, and the man sees no
Colours or anything,
Being easy only in things of the mind,
The child is easy in feeling.

154

Easy in feeling, easily excessive
And in excess powerful,
For instance, if you do not speak to the child
He will make trouble.

You would say a man had the upper hand
Of the child, if a child survive,
I say the child has fingers of strength
To strangle the man alive.

Oh it is not happy, it is never happy,
To carry the child into adulthood,
Let children lie down before full growth
And die in their infanthood

And be guilty of no man's blood.

But oh the poor child, the poor child, what can he do,
Trapped in a grown-up carapace,
But peer outside of his prison room
With the eye of an anarchist?

Mutchmore and Not-So

THE big family
In our parts
Are the Likelies
(A cousin of mine married one of them)
They have a large house called Mutchmore
Standing in well-wooded grounds,
A beautiful place, dating
In the front hall and lower part of the fire-place
From the days of Henry the Eighth.
In this house
Now alone since his wife died
And the girls married
Lives Sefton the head of the family.
We always called him Mutchmore Likely
To distinguish him from Gerald.
Gerald Likely is the son
Of old Sir Sefton's younger brother
(Nobody thought much of *him*).
Gerald is not on speaking terms with his Uncle
Ever since he changed the name of *his* house

Such a pretty little Georgian house
Fronting on the High Street
As you come into Mutch village
Opposite the church yard
(You cannot see the church because
Of the left-hand turn to the mill house)
Changed the name of *his* house
From Parkins to Not-So.
Gerald has such a *peculiar* sense of humour;
Why should that old rascal Sefton,
He used to say,
Preen himself, the unlovable old character,
On what he fondly imagines to be
The lovable nickname of Mutchmore?
So you see, he, Gerald, thought he would
Take away from the pleasure his uncle took in his nickname,
Spite him, really, by calling his own house Not-So.
Mutchmore Likely and now Not-So Likely!
Of course we had to laugh,
But it made the whole thing ridiculous,
Which is what Gerald wanted.
The old man may have his faults
But Gerald is really too ill-natured.

The Last Turn of the Screw

I am Miles, I did not die
I only turned, as on shut eye
To feel again the silken dress
Of my lovely governess.

Yes, it was warm, poetical and cosy,
I never saw the other fellow when
I lolled on Lady's lap (I called her Lady)
But there were two of us all right. And both were men.

Yes, there's the oddest part. She made me feel
A hundred years more old than I was, than she was,
She'd had a sheltered life, of course—a vicarage,
Some bustling younger children, a father pious, I'm sure he
    was.

But two of us? Of me? I'll be explicit,
A soft boy, knowing rather more than boys should, lolling,
No harm in that, on Lady's lap; the other,
Source of my knowledge, half my self by now, but calling . . .

Some children are born innocent, some achieve it,
You scowl; that doesn't fit with your philosophy?
Can you by choosing alter Nature, you inquire?
Yes, my dear sir, you can; I found it fairly easy.

But calling (to go back a step) but calling?—
That proved he was not yet quite One of Us,
The vulgar little beast, the fellow Quint.
It was at first my lordly feelings held him off
That dapper knowingness of his for instance,
The clothes right, being my uncle's, but worn wrong,
The accent careful, well he must be careful,
I dare say he had thumbed a book about it . . .
To spend ten minutes with a Thing like this

Would be too long.
So snobbery made the breach, religion followed . . .
Ten minutes? No, Eternity, with Quint
That Quint, whose seedy sickness in my blood
I could detect (in time?) running to flood,
The sickliness of sin,
Oh yes, I saw quite plain by now
What was going in.
How did I fob him off? (now we know why)
When half my heart
Was panting for him and what he could teach
Reaching for shame, and retching too
(It was, as I have said, this squeamishness I had
First judged him bad).

Oh there was still some rotting to go on
In my own heart
Before I was quite ready to cry 'Out!'
And see him off, though half my blood went with him.
I grow a shade dramatic here, none went at all,
My sinews have remained the same, my blood, my heart
Have not, as I'm aware, taken a taint,
I was not and I am not now a saint,
But I loved Virtue, and I love her still,
Especially as I see her in the dress
Of my sweetly fatheaded governess . . .
Well, let's be plain, I fobbed Quint off
By simply failing to be clever enough.
By taking nothing in, not looking and not noticing
I made myself as dull to the persuading
Of all that shabby innuendo as
The plainest ten-year schoolboy ever was,
And so I have remained and by intent
Quite dull. And shall remain
Sooner than chance such entering again.

I did not die, but bought my innocence
At the high price of an indifference
Where once I knew the most engaging love
That first through squeamishness made virtue move,
The love, now lost of my sweet governess
Who cannot bear I should be so much less
The Miles she knew, or rather did not know.
Yes, I have lost my interestingness for Lady who,
I fear, like other innocent ladies do,
Hankered for something shady,
Well, say, dramatic, not what I am now,
An empty antic Clumsy, a mere boy.
She'll never know
The strength I have employed and do employ
To make it sure
I shall be this
And nothing more.
I am Miles, I did not die,
I only turn, as on shut eye
To feel again the silken dress
Of my lost and lovely governess,
And sigh and think it strange
That being dull I should feel so much pain.

Company

RISE from your bed of languor
Rise from your bed of dismay
Your friends will not come tomorrow
As they did not come today

You must rely on yourself, they said,
You must rely on yourself,
Oh but I find this pill so bitter said the poor man
As he took it from the shelf

Crying, Oh sweet Death come to me
Come to me for company,
Sweet Death it is only you I can
Constrain for company.

Saffron

UNDERNEATH the ice
Lies the frozen spirit of Bice

Green are her eyes, green her hair,
The spirit of Bice is winter's prisoner.

When spring comes Pale is her name, and her hair
And eyes are pale blue, and she is freer.

In summertime she is called Saffron,
Yellow are eyes and hair then. I welcome

Bice, Pale and Saffron but I love best
Beautiful summer Saffron, running fast.

Because this beautiful spirit should not be frozen
And is furthest from it when she is saffron.

Avondale

How sweet the birds of Avondale
Of Avondale, of Avondale,
How sweet the birds of Avondale
Do swoop and swing and call.

The children too of Avondale,
Of Avondale, of Avondale,
The boys and girls of Avondale
Do swoop and swing and call,

And all the little cats and dogs,
Of Avondale, of Avondale,
In their own way in Avondale
Do swoop and swing and call,

And oh it is a pleasant sight
It is a very pleasant sight
To see the creatures so delight
To swoop and swing and call,
In Avondale, in Avondale,
To see them swoop and call.

Avondall

I HAD a dream I was a bird
A bird of Avondall
Sitting with birds upon a roof
To swoop and swing and call
I was athirst with other birds
To swoop and swing and call
But no bird turned to me in love
All were inimical,
They were inimical.

Valuable
(After reading two paragraphs in a newspaper)

ALL these illegitimate babies . . .
Oh girls, girls,
Silly little cheap things,
Why do you not put some value on yourselves,
Learn to say, No?
Did nobody teach you?
Nobody teaches anybody to say No nowadays,
People should teach people to say No.

Oh poor panther,
Oh you poor black animal,
At large for a few moments in a school for young children in
    Paris,
Now in your cage again,
How your great eyes bulge with bewilderment,
There is something there that accuses us,
In your angry and innocent eyes,
Something that says:
I am too valuable to be kept in a cage.

Oh these illegitimate babies!
Oh girls, girls,
Silly little valuable things,
You should have said, No, I am valuable,
And again, It is because I am valuable
I say, No.

Nobody teaches anybody they are valuable nowadays.

Girls, you are valuable,
And you, Panther, you are valuable,
But the girls say: I shall be alone
If I say 'I am valuable' and other people do not say it of me,
I shall be alone, there is no comfort there.
No, it is not comforting but it is valuable,
And if everybody says it in the end
It will be comforting. And for the panther too,
If everybody says he is valuable
It will be comforting for him.

I Wish

Oh I wish that there were some wing, some wing,
Under which I could hide my head,
A soft grey wing, a beautiful thing,
Oh I wish that there were such a wing,

And then I should suddenly be quite sure
As I never was before,
And fly far away, and be gay instead
Of being hesitating and filled with dread,
Oh I wish I could find a wing.

But today as I walk on the pavement I see
Where a car is parked, where a car is parked,
In the wheel's bright chromium hub I see
A world stretching out that is like but unlike
The world that encloses me.

And I wish to pass through the shining hub
And go far away, far away,
As far as I might on the wings of the dove
That first I thought would succour me
And carry me far away,
Oh the hub is my love far more than the dove
That first I thought would succour me.

And now the shining beautiful hub
Opens its door to me,
I enter, I enter, through the hub I have entered
The world that shines so bright,
The road stretches there in ochre; and blue
Is the sky I am walking into; and white
Is the beach I perceive of a heavenly sea
A-roll in the realms of light,
It rolls in the realms of light.

The Listener

LISTENING one day on the radio
To 'An encounter with mosquitoes in New Guinea' by Miss
    Cheeseman,
I fell to thinking of the animal kingdom
And experienced at once a relief of nervous tension.
For I thought, Their battles are as ours, as ours,
They are no different from our own,
Then rose up a Spirit from the ether that touched my eyelids
And cast me in a deep swoon.

Hymn to the Seal

(To the tune: 'Soldiers of Christ, arise!'
Hymns Ancient & Modern)

CREATURE of God, thy coat
That lies all black and fine
I do admire, as on a sunny
Rock to see thee climb.

When thou wast young thy coat
Was pale with spots upon it,
But now in single black it lies
And thou, Seal, liest on it.

What bliss abounds to view
God's creatures in their prime
Climb in full coat upon a rock
To breathe and to recline.

171

Fish Fish

Look, man, look,
Underneath the brook
Sits the fish fish
On a hook.

What, man, what?
Let him off?
No fear fear
I'm going to look.

Yes, now I think I will go down to him,
To have a look at him,
In the depths
Of the perishable brook.

So go now man, pray go,
No more say
Loose the fish fish from the hook
To swim away.

Underneath the brook dim
Sits the fish,
He sits *on* the hook
It is not *in* him.

He is waiting for me
To carry me to the sea
I shall be happy then
In the watery company of his kingdom.

Goodbye, man dear,
Goodbye quickly,
I go to the fish fish
Impatiently.

Venus When Young Choosing Death

I stood knee-deep in the sea
I saw gods coming towards me
All came and kissed, all kissed
It was for friendship.

It was a hot day
The sea
Lapped to my knees
And kissed me.

All the gods were old friends
I knew them from long ago
They kissed me each after each and went
In friendship,

Kissed me on the lips
Held me to them
Set me again in the knee-deep sea
And went, in friendship.

Then came one drawing a boat after him
He set me in the boat
He set me on his knees in the boat, kissing me.
It was not for friendship.

Oh how happy this day was
All day in his arms I was,
But not for friendship.

A little breeze drew now from the land
Bringing a smell of poppies
And on his head, was poppies
And in his hand, poppies
And on his lips when he kissed me
A taste of poppies.

Sleep or Death, Sleep or Death kissed me,
Not for friendship.

You do not kiss one for friendship?
No, for welcome,
To welcome one home.

Lord Say-and-Seal

LORD Say-and-Seal, Lord Say-and-Seal
Why not for once say and *reveal*
All the dark thoughts your words go over
To make a pretty bog-hole cover.

The Days of Yore

WHAT pleased him more
Than anything else
Was the resemblance he bore
To the Prince of Wales,

To the Prince of Wales
And more and more
As the Prince of Wales was
In the days of yore.

Pearl

(To an American lady poet committing suicide because of not being appreciated enough)

THEN cried the American poet where she lay supine:
'My name is Purrel; I was caast before swine.'

Yes, I know

THAT pale face stretches across the centuries
It is so subtle and yielding; yet innocent,
Her name is Lucretia Borgia.

Yes, I know. I knew her brother Cesare
Once. But only for a short time.

Widowhood
or
The Home-Coming of Lady Ross
(Her husband, the Lord of the Isles, is dead, and she lives alone
by the sea)

NOBODY hears me, nobody sees me,
My father, the General, used to say
He had only to come into a room
For everybody else to go out of it.

('Ach, wie schrecklich, so alt zu sein,
    Und diese schrecklichen Tränensäcke,
    Als wenn sie viel geweint hätte!'
Said the young girl to her friend,
In the hotel at Baden.)

My heart is a frozen lump,
I look forward to nothing but Death,
I am glad Harold is not here
To see me now.

('Oh how awful, to be so old,
    And those awful tear-tracks on her cheeks,
    As if she had cried a lot!'
Said the young girl to her friend
In the hotel at Cheltenham.)

Harold loved the hotel at Baden and the hotel at Cheltenham
He loved staying in hotels, he loved staying in 'em.

Now I live alone by the sea
And I am happy as never I used to be,
Harold, can you forgive me?
My family were never much good in company.

That's what you used to say, dear, do you remember, when I
    stayed in my room
In the hotel at Baden, or wherever it might be, Up you would
    come
Rushing, and kiss me and cry: Rhoda, your family,
I must say, are not much good in company.

Oh Harold, our house looks so beautiful today,
Why did you always want to go away?

Voice from the Tomb (1)
(Nightmare, after reading The Parable of the Talents)

HERE lies a poet who would not write
His soul runs screaming through the night
Oh give me paper, give me pen,
And I will very soon begin.

Poor Soul, keep silent; in Death's clime
There's no pen, paper, notion,
And no Time.

Voice from the Tomb (2)
(To the tune: 'From Greenland's icy mountains',
Hymns A. & M.)

I TROD a foreign path, dears,
The silence was extreme
And so it came about, dears,
That I fell into dream,

That I fell into dream, my dear,
And feelings beyond cause,
And tears without a reason
And so was lost.

Voice from the Tomb (3)

SUCH evidence I have of indifference
Were surely enough to break the coldest heart,
But this heart is not cold, it never has been cold,
It never, never, never has been cold.

Voice from the Tomb (4)

I DIED for lack of company
Did my dear friends not know?
Oh why would they not speak to me
Yet said they loved me so?

Voice from the Tomb (5)
(A Soul earthbound by the grievance of never having been
important)

YOU never heard of me, I dare
Say. Well, I'm here.

182

The Dedicated Dancing Bull and the Water Maid
(Beethoven's Sonata in F, Op. 17, for Horn and Piano,
played by Dennis Brain and Denis Matthews)

Hop hop, thump thump,
Oh I am holy, oh I am plump,
A young bull dancing on the baked grass glade,
And beside me dances the Water Maid.
She says I must dance with her,
Why should I? I loathe her,
She has such a stupid way of singing
It does not amount to anything,
But she thinks it does, oh yes
She does not suppose she is spurious.
I wish I could be rid of the Water Maid
Or hid from her. Does she think she can make me afraid?
Ho ho, thump thump,
Oh I am elegant, oh I am plump,
As I wave my head my feet go thud
On the baked grass. Oh I am good.
Now night comes and I go into the wood shades
And the moon comes up and lights them as the day fades.

Hop hop, faster faster,
Thump thump, but the Maid comes after,
She is teasing me by singing with a stupid sound
That does not go at all well with my bound,
Oh how I should like to tread her in the ground.
But I must think only about my feet
And remember to bring them down on the beat.
Hoo hoo, now I sing through my nose,
Hoo hoo, and off the Maid goes
A little way in an affected flutter
Pretending to be startled by the hoo of my deep mutter.
Hoo, then, hoo, with a hop and a jump
Who is this beautiful young animal who is so plump?
Why it is our famous dedicated dancing bull,
Did you notice how delicately he goes?
Was that a hoof somewhere in those silver toes?
With nonsense
The Water Maid makes off into the distance.
The night is mine now and I come to the forest pool
   And drink and do not think I am a fool.

Night Thoughts

THERE were thoughts that came to Phil
And Oh they made him feel quite ill,

They were so envious and bitter,
He wished he could have something sweeter,

But still he felt it was all right
As long as they only came by night.

He thought about his job . . . so dull,
And poorly paid; all that was awful,

And then his girl, he loved her very much,
Only she did not seem to love him quite so much.

As for friends—Phil groaned aloud,
His thoughts drove in like a night-cloud,

But still it *was* night, and so he felt
It was just something that could not be helped.

The thoughts however by now were single-minded,
They did not fuss or beat around it,

They simply tried to find a way
To make it seem they came by day.

When at last they succeeded in doing this
Poor Phil adopted a most peculiar neurosis,

He summoned up a picture of shallow sea-water
And in it he paddled, he was a sea-walker.

On an empty beach, in full sun,
He paddled for miles and did not see anyone,

And as he walked, the salty smell and the air
Of the beautiful place, *worked*; he did not remember.

That beach, as a matter of fact, shelves to deep water,
He must be careful to remain always a coastal-walker.

Happy Phil in his solitude. I am glad
He has this retreat. But it is not good.

Piggy to Joey

PIGGY to Joey,
Piggy to Joe,
Yes, that's what I was—
Piggy to Joe.

Will he come back again?
Oh no, no, no.
Oh how I wish I hadn't been
Piggy to Joe.

Pretty

WHY is the word pretty so underrated?
In November the leaf is pretty when it falls
The stream grows deep in the woods after rain
And in the pretty pool the pike stalks

He stalks his prey, and this is pretty too,
The prey escapes with an underwater flash
But not for long, the great fish has him now
The pike is a fish who always has his prey

And this is pretty. The water rat is pretty
His paws are not webbed, he cannot shut his nostrils
As the otter can and the beaver, he is torn between
The land and water. Not 'torn', he does not mind.

The owl hunts in the evening and it is pretty
The lake water below him rustles with ice
There is frost coming from the ground, in the air mist
All this is pretty, it could not be prettier.

Yes, it could always be prettier, the eye abashes
It is becoming an eye that cannot see enough,
Out of the wood the eye climbs. This is prettier
A field in the evening, tilting up.

The field tilts to the sky. Though it is late
The sky is lighter than the hill field
All this looks easy but really it is extraordinary
Well, it is extraordinary to be so pretty.

And it is careless, and that is always pretty
This field, this owl, this pike, this pool are careless,
As Nature is always careless and indifferent
Who sees, who steps, means nothing, and this is pretty.

So a person can come along like a thief—pretty!—
Stealing a look, pinching the sound and feel,
Lick the icicle broken from the bank
And still say nothing at all, only cry pretty.

Cry pretty, pretty, pretty and you'll be able
Very soon not even to cry pretty
And so be delivered entirely from humanity
This is prettiest of all, it is very pretty.

The Small Lady

In front of the mighty washing machine
The small lady stood in a beautiful dream,
'That these clothes so clean (oh what a relief)
   Must still be ironed, is my only grief.'

But then came a great witch passing on the air
Who said, 'What is it you still wish for, my pretty dear?
Would you like to be a duck on a northern lake,
A milky white duck with a yellow beak?'
'Aroint thee, false witch!' cried the lady with a brave face,
'Human inventions help properly, magic is a disgrace.'
The witch flew off cackling for the harm was done,
'I smell water,' cried the lady and followed her into the
      setting sun.
And now in a false shape, on the wind-driven black pelt
Of that far northern lake, she is without help:
Crying, Away, away,
Come, ray of the setting sun,
Over the lake
Spread thy red streak,
Light my kingdom.

Heart of my heart, it is a mournful song,
Never will this poor lady come home.

Animula, vagula, blandula
(The Emperor Hadrian to his soul)

LITTLE soul so sleek and smiling
Flesh's friend and guest also
Where departing will you wander
Growing paler now and languid
And not joking as you used to?

Friends of the River Trent
(At their Annual Dinner)

A DWINDLING body of ageing fish
Is all we can present
Because of water pollution
In the River Trent
Because of water pollution, my boys,
And a lack of concerted action,
These fish of what they used to be
Is only a measly fraction
A-swimming about most roomily
Where they shoved each other before,
Yet not beefing about being solitary
Or the sparseness of the fare.
Then three cheers for the ageing fish, my boys,
Content in polluted depths
To grub up enough food, my boys,
To carry 'em to a natural death,
And may we do the same, my boys,
And carry us to a natural death.

Is it Happy?

Is it happy for me, is it happy
That my father, Lord Beale, was so famous
And I am a ne'er-do-weel? Is it happy?

And what of my mother—'the lady'
We called her, because she was so high-minded, born
        Plaidy—
Was it happy for her
That Father was never there?
Was it happy?

And Rory, Rory my brother
Who knew neither father nor brother
Being adopted in infancy by Uncle Pym
Whose name he took, was it happy for him?

Thorwald, our spaniel, gun-trained,
Died of a fatty heart;
Well, Father was never at home,
And I didn't shoot.
Was it happy for Thorwald?

. . . all that money paid out for a worthless scrip
That might have been mine today
If Papa had stuck to Gilt Edged or Blue Chip,
Is that happy?

My father died in his fame
Saving his country and me
From the people over the sea.
How does it feel being Beale,
Lord Beale and a ne'er-do-weel?

I've brought Mother home to the little house,
Having let the grand one for a commando course,
Telling 'em to look out for the pictures, of course.

All my life I have tried not to be envious
Of Father, or take it out by being nefarious,
Truly I loved him, revere
The memory of this great soldier,
Field Marshall Lord B. he was when he died,
(Happy, for me?)

Mother says I should bring home a bride,
Greatness skips a generation, she says, and he,
My son, need not be a nonentity.

I'll do it, why not?
Play the part out,
Find a sort of happiness in it too I dare say, slyly
Being as it were all this quite so entirely,
Blithely calling the saviour of my country, Father,
(Happy for me)
Blithely begetting sons to carry it farther,
(Will that be?)

I'll ask Cynthia tonight, she'll say yes,
When I've got the Commandos out she'll love the place.

It's occurred to me also once or twice of late
To join the True Church, something Father would hate,
Not the Anglicans of course, they're too humdrum,
It would have to be the Roman Communion.
Well, I've read Father Gerard and about the recusants quite
    a lot
And can prove: *As they suffered*, there cannot have been a
    Catholic Plot.

Is it happy for me, driving Mother mad?
Does she wish I was bad?
Think Rory might have been better than me?
Well, if she does, she don't let me see.

Happy, is it happy?

Watchful
(A Tale of Psyche)

WHEN Watchful came to me he said
As he never said before,
Wait, wait, I will see you
On Northumberland Moor.

I played with my brothers
In Northumberland House
And we laughed as we skipped and ran
And made a great noise,

And I looked through the window
And saw the sea run white
Against Northumberland,
Country of my delight.

When Watchful spoke,
As he never used to speak,
I drew apart from my brothers,
I scowled to hear Watchful speak,

Come to me, come to me,
Upon Northumberland Moor, hurry!
I will not come yet
But I will come some day.

First I must play with my brothers
And make some money
On the Stock Exchange. It was funny
How we made so much money
Because we did not want it in the old
Tall house in Northumberland,
In fact we did not want it much at all.

Often we gave parties
In London
For Senior Civil Servants
And barristers
And Junior Members
Of the Government.

I said to my brother Tommy,
It is funny
How they come
When we do not want them very much.

Tommy said, It is funny
Like the money,
We do not want
It or them very much,
Yet they come.

It is funny, Tommy, too, I said,
How the warmth of the parties
Fascinates me, and the wild laughing eyes
Of the people hold me.

You would not have thought
That the people we had
At our parties would have
These wild laughing eyes, but they had.

Watch out, said Tommy, the word is Watchful,
Then
We were in Northumberland again.

The window of our schoolroom was open
And in the group of my brothers in the room was one,
      quickly,
Who was not a brother, coming to me.

I climbed down from the window in the high moonlight
Along the high brick wall of the kitchen garden
I crawled. But the wall was higher
Than I remembered it was. So when I went to drop
Off the high wall, where we used to by the mulberry tree,
It was suddenly too high, I hung by my fingers above a
      precipice,
But I could not hang long, I let go, I fell, fell far, fell,
Was caught. I stiffened in the arms that held me, slipped
      down and ran free.

Over the saltings I ran. The midnight high wind
Pulled my straight hair in streaks behind me, and I ran and
      ran
And did not care, as I ran by the sea shore
If Watchful ran behind or waited for me
On Northumberland Moor.

Oh how strongly the wind drew. When day broke
The waves leapt and their crests ran gold
In the morning sun, the gold sun was in their crests.

Turn away, turn away
From the high crests of the golden sea,
It was funny
How easily I turned away from the high crests, as easily
As from the parties
And the money.

I was running in a wood now, a wood of pine trees,
Very dark it was and silent, I ran on brown pine needles
Silently, and came to a gamekeeper's gallows. The mournful
    birds
Hanging there cried: We are not Watchful, and an old
    badger
Crawling to his sett to die said: I am not Watchful. But the
    wind
Cried: Hurry! and drove great snowflakes against my face.
Then I came to a dark house and the door swung and I
    went in,
Oh Watchful, my darling, you have led me such a dance.

He lay on a truckle bed, cold, cold; his eyes shut.

First I made a fire from the wood stacked and the pine
    cones,
Then I came back to him, Oh Watchful, you are so cold,
So I lay on him to warm him, and by and by
He opened his eyes and laughed to see me cry.

We need not dance any more
He said, Only the fire dances on Northumberland Moor,
The fire you have lighted for me dances
On Northumberland Moor.

Then winter blew away, a sweet sea ran pretty
And in this new world everything was happy.

How Cruel is the Story of Eve

How cruel is the story of Eve
What responsibility
It has in history
For cruelty.

Touch, where the feeling is most vulnerable,
Unblameworthy—ah reckless—desiring children,
Touch there with a touch of pain?
Abominable.

Ah what cruelty,
In history
What misery.

Put up to barter
The tender feelings
Buy her a husband to rule her
Fool her to marry a master
She must or rue it
The Lord said it.

And man, poor man,
Is he fit to rule,
Pushed to it?
How can he carry it, the governance,
And not suffer for it
Insuffisance?
He must make woman lower then
So he can be higher then.

Oh what cruelty,
In history what misery.

Soon woman grows cunning
Masks her wisdom,
How otherwise will he
Bring food and shelter, kill enemies?
If he did not feel superior
It would be worse for her
And for the tender children
Worse for them.

Oh what cruelty,
In history what misery
Of falsity.

It is only a legend
You say? But what
Is the meaning of the legend
If not
To give blame to women most
And most punishment?

This is the meaning of a legend that colours
All human thought; it is not found among animals.

How cruel is the story of Eve,
What responsibility it has
In history
For misery.

Yet there is this to be said still:
Life would be over long ago
If men and women had not loved each other
Naturally, naturally,
Forgetting their mythology
They would have died of it else
Long ago, long ago,
And all would be emptiness now
And silence.

Oh dread Nature, for your purpose,
To have made them love so.

The Story I Have Told

I SAW the ghostly lady fleeting
In imperial purple clad
Through the trees of Lost Oleela
By the slopes of Morgenstad,

Where a carven pillar stood up,
White as bone, as white as bone,
Paused the lady, weeping paused she,
Laid her hand upon the stone,
There with fixèd mien awhile
She stood, and vanished with a moan.

Then spake a voice within my bosom
Answering what I had not asked:
You have seen the lady Fausta
Who in life was overtasked

Overtasked to seek a daughter,
Seek the lovely Eulalie,
Daily comes she, daily pauses,
Seeking Eulalie.

Eulalie beloved daughter,
A fair child and lost,
Close were they to one another
In misfortune crossed,

It was the Emperor Eelogab
Who sent them both away,
A daughter fair, a virtuous wife,
A deed to darken day,
He sent them forth to live or die
For all it happened had,
Beside the trees of Lost Oleel'
And the slopes of Morgenstad,
In castle grim and sad.

Often through the groves at midnight
Eulalie alone
Gathered moonflowers to her breast
And tarried by the stone.

In a white dress tarried she,
Sashed with violet,
In a white dress sashed with violet
Tarried Eulalie.

Until one night a sullen storm,
A storm of deep intent,
Caught her up and carried her
And never home she went.

Never home went Eulalie
In her dress of white
And the lady Fausta waited
For her this and every night,
Waited for her, weeping for her,
This and every night.

The lady Fausta long is dead
Though she may weep and crave,
But Eulalie, fair Eulalie,
She lies not in the grave.

Ah me, what changèd voice is this
That was so soft and sad,
That now cries: Fear Oleela's grove
And the slopes of Morgenstad,
That bids me flee Oleela's grove
And the slopes of Morgenstad.

There is no place in all the world
Where I shall not behold
The lady Fausta weeping, pause
As she paused in days of old,
Beside the stone whose sides are carved
With the story I have told,

Of Fausta and of Eulalie,
The story I have told.

Fairy Story

I WENT into the wood one day
And there I walked and lost my way

When it was so dark I could not see
A little creature came to me

He said if I would sing a song
The time would not be very long

But first I must let him hold my hand tight
Or else the wood would give me a fright

I sang a song, he let me go
But now I am home again there is nobody I know.

Angel Face

ANGEL face so close above me
In the snowflake glowing smugly
Sweet Angel, love me, love me.

White and silent is the snowflake
Falling, falling, and it will make
Soon all flat and like a white lake
In a white and silent state
Beaming flat and vacant.

But thy face will beckon, beckon,
Saying to me, Come soon, come soon,
As is thy snowy custom
It is thy snowy custom

When at night the flakes are falling
Of the midnight snowstorm falling

To be so appealing, teasing
Smiling, teasing and appealing,
In thy white and silent way
Saying only, Come away.

If I doubt thee, if I think thee
But a figment of my fancy,
Sweet Angel, love me, love me,
In thy bosom cover me.

The Grange

Oh there hasn't been much change
At the Grange,

Of course the blackberries growing closer
Make getting in a bit of a poser,
But there hasn't been much change
At the Grange.

Old Sir Prior died,
They say on the point of leaving for the seaside,
They never found the body, which seemed odd to some
(Not me, seeing as what I seen the butler done.)

Oh there hasn't been much change
At the Grange.

The governess 'as got it now,
Miss Ursy 'aving moved down to the Green Cow—
Proper done out of 'er rights, she was, a b. shame.
And what's that the governess pushes round at nights in the
        old pram?

Oh there hasn't been much change
At the Grange.

The shops leave supplies at the gate now, meat, groceries,
Mostly old tinned stuff you know from McInnes's,
They wouldn't go up to the door,
Not after what happened to Fred's pa.

Oh there hasn't been much change
At the Grange.

Parssing there early this morning, cor lummy,
I 'ears a whistling sound coming from the old chimney,
Whistling it was fit to bust and not a note wrong,
The old pot, whistling The Death of Nelson.

No there hasn't been much change
At the Grange,

But few goes that way somehow,
Not now.

'I believe.'   *'I do not.'*

Mrs Arbuthnot

MRS ARBUTHNOT was a poet
A poet of high degree,
But her talent left her;
Now she lives at home by the sea.

In the morning she washes up,
In the afternoon she sleeps,
Only in the evenings sometimes
For her lost talent she weeps,

Crying: I should write a poem,
Can I look a wave in the face
If I do not write a poem about a sea-wave,
Putting the words in place.

Mrs Arbuthnot has died,
She has gone to heaven,
She is one with the heavenly combers now
And need not write about them.

Cry: She is a heavenly comber,
She runs with a comb of fire,
Nobody writes or wishes to
Who is one with their desire.

Magnificent Words

('Ye shall be a blessing; fear not, but let your hands
be strong.'—Zech. VIII, 13.)

THESE magnificent words that I read today
Are what the Daily Telegraph had chosen, to display
From the bible.

Who is it who chooses at the Daily Telegraph each day
Magnificent words out of all of them, to display
From the bible?

This unknown person's hand is strong, he is a blessing,
Everyday
He chooses magnificent words in the Daily Telegraph, to
display
From the bible.

So can anger . . .

THEY do not come separately
They are never alone
They come all together
Or they stay at home

I liked one of them,
I asked one,
But he laughed and said: You forget
Our name is Legion.

All right, stay away then,
If I have to have the others as well.

So can anger sometimes
Save us from hell.

On Walking Slowly After an Accident

I USED to walk quickly
But now I walk slow
I see the sunshine on each leaf
And the spider below.

I know the spider
I know his trick
I see the web shake
As he gives a kick

And I see that the fly he goes for
Is not a fly but a dandelion seed,
He harvests with chagrin
What cannot feed.

I turn to the sunny leaf
From the chagrin below
Knowing never a spider, poor spider,
Could so,

Nor a quick walker either
For he would have seen neither
Leaf nor spider, leaf nor spider,

Ni le chagrin de dandelion seed.

I am a girl who loves to shoot

I AM a girl who loves to shoot,
I love the feathered fowl and brute,
I love them with a love as strong
As ever there came from heaven down.

Why should I not love them living as dead?
As I shoot, as I shoot, and as my fine dog Tray
Brings the shot one to hand, he is I, I am they.
Oh why do my friends think this love is so questionable?
They say they love animals but they do not love them as I
     am able,

Seeing them run and fly and letting them run, fly and die,
I love them to distraction as the wild wind goes by,
As the rain and the storm on this wide upper hill,
Oh no one loves the animals as I do or so well.
If I am not hungry I let them run free,
And if I am hungry they are my darling passionate delicacy.

Into the wild woods I go over the high mountain to the
    valley low,
And the animals are safe; if I am not hungry they may run
    and go,
And I bless their beautiful appearance and their fleetness,
And I feel no contradiction or contriteness.
I love them living and I love them dead with a quick blood
    spurt
And I may put them in the pot and eat them up with a
    loving heart.

I am a girl who loves to shoot,
I love the feathered fowl and brute,
I love them with as great a love
As ever came down from heaven above.

I love . . .

I LOVE the English country scene
But sometimes think there's too much Hooker's green,
Especially in August, when the flowers that might have lent a
Lightness, don't; being gamboge or magenta.

Cœur Simple

WHERE is the sky hurrying to
Over my head,
Mother, is the sky hurrying
To bed?

Where is the sky hurrying to
Over my head?
Where it will be hurrying to
When you are dead.

Nodding

TIZDAL my beautiful cat
Lies on the old rag mat
In front of the kitchen fire.
Outside the night is black.

The great fat cat
Lies with his paws under him
His whiskers twitch in a dream,
He is slumbering.

The clock on the mantelpiece
Ticks unevenly, tic toc, tic-toc,
Good heavens what is the matter
With the kitchen clock?

Outside an owl hunts,
Hee hee hee hee,
Hunting in the Old Park
From his snowy tree.
What on earth can he find in the park tonight,
It is so wintry?

Now the fire burns suddenly too hot
Tizdal gets up to move,
Why should such an animal
Provoke our love?

The twigs from the elder bush
Are tapping on the window pane
As the wind sets them tapping,
Now the tapping begins again.

One laughs on a night like this
In a room half firelight half dark
With a great lump of a cat
Moving on the hearth,
And the twigs tapping quick,
And the owl in an absolute fit
One laughs supposing creation
Pays for its long plodding
Simply by coming to this—
Cat, night, fire—and a girl nodding.

v.

ADELA is such a silly woman
Tom says Adela is going off her head

Adela is staying down in the country
She is v. happy

Dr Not is v. nice

Such a jolly old place quite like home

Dr Not is v. nice
Adela is v. happy

Adela is Not is
v. v. happy

With extensive grounds.

A British Song

It was a slender British bird
Stood on the drinking bath
But another came and nipped him there
Before he could have a bath.

Then came a great British starling, nipped the nipper and
  drove him away
And sat down in the bath, and sat down in the bath. And
  there did stay.

When the wind . . .

WHEN the wind is in the East
I give a feast

When the wind is in the West
I rest

When the wind is in the South
There is a taste of sugar in my mouth

When the wind is North
I go not forth.

By the spread Arabian table
Sit the friends whom I am able
To arouse. They come to me
Across the pink Arabian sea.

I like to sleep beneath my canopy
The sun reaches to me
By the silent sea on the sands
The tropical evening sun reaches to me.

Heavy the scent of bees, heavy the sun
Heavy the taste of sugar on my tongue
Heavy the days, will they never pass?
Heavy my sleep, will it come at last?

It is winter now: the wind howls
The snowy fox and the snowy owls
Hunt in the night. I stay within.
Outside my house I hear the storms begin.

Which winds did I like best?
Why, the East and the West,
They brought me tranquillity
The others, anxiety.

Northumberland House

I was always a thoughtful youngster,
Said the lady on the omnibus,
I remember Father used to say:
You are more thoughtful than us.

I was sensitive too, the least thing
Upset me so much,
I used to cry if a fly
Stuck in the hatch.

Mother always said:
Elsie is too good,
There'll never be another like Elsie,
Touch wood.

I liked to be alone
Sitting on the garden path,
My brother said he'd never seen a
Picture more like Faith in the Arena.

They were kindly people, my people,
I could not help being different,
And I think it was good for me
Mixing in a different element.

The poor lady now burst out crying
And I saw her friend was not a friend but a nurse
For she said, Cheer up duckie the next stop is ours,
They got off at Northumberland House.

This great House of the Percys
Is now a lunatic asylum,
But over the gate there still stands
The great Northumberland Lion.

This family animal's tail
Is peculiar in that it is absolutely straight,
And straight as a bar it stood out to drop after them
As they went through the gate.

The Crown of Gold

(An English Writer in Search of an Established English
Publisher)

MOTHER procure for me a golden crown
Said the child, That the fire may not burn me nor the seas
　　drown.

She took the child and ran for three years in the wilderness
　　with him.
And beside them ran a German-Jewish man
And he loved the child and protected him
Crying: Remember Jerusalem.
And he crowned the child with a crown of affection.

But the child said
Mother, it is not a crown of affection I want
It is a crown of gold.

And the child and his mother ran more quickly in the
　　wilderness
And more quickly beside them ran the German-Jewish man
Crying: Remember Jerusalem.
And he said, Nobody has loved your child as I have loved him.

And the child said, Mother procure for me a crown of gold
You are not required to think about anything else.

And the German-Jewish man kissed the crowned child's hand
　　as he ran
Crying: Remember Jerusalem.

And the child stood in the path
And he took from his head the crown of affection
And threw it at the feet of the German-Jewish man
Crying: Remember Jerusalem.

And they left the German-Jewish man and left the wilderness
And she procured for her child a crown of gold
And they sat in a pleasant garden in a fine city.

And the child said, Mother, gold is the right material for a
    crown
It is only in the wilderness that crowns of affection are worn,
And she said, No it is not and began to weep and wring her
    hands,
Do not be foolish Mother, he said, I am no longer young.
And she said, Remember Jerusalem.

And the wind blew strong and rattled the leaves of the
    poplar trees
And the child did not hear, or heard and laughed, he did not
    care
But the strong wind took the words and carried them to the
    wilderness
Where they fell to the ground in a dry place.
And the mother of the child stopped crying and was resigned
    to the golden crown
And she said, Now may the fire not burn my child nor the
    seas drown.

Why do I . . .

WHY do I think of Death as a friend?
It is because he is a scatterer
He scatters the human frame
The nerviness and the great pain
Throws it on the fresh fresh air
And now it is nowhere
Only sweet Death does this
Sweet Death, kind Death,
Of all the gods you are best.

Some Are Born

SOME are born to peace and joy
And some are born to sorrow
But only for a day as we
Shall not be here tomorrow.

Saint Anthony and the Rose of Life
A Desert Vision

A DARK rose grew in the desert
A red and velvety flower
And opened her petals one by one
In the midnight hour.

Her leaves were a beautiful bright dark green
And this might only be seen
Because the full moon riding high
Threw a delicate beam.

The rose grew in a sand
Of a horrible grey yellow
For the moon that had made the red rose red
Made the sand sallow.

A strapping life heavy and bright
Bulged in the rose and her leaves
And up from the roots of the substantial plant
The bold drops ran like thieves.

Like burly thieves in a shadowy night
In a night of profound shades
They have carried aloft the colours of life
To flaunt in the deathly glades.

Oh rose oh leaves so much alive
What are you doing here,
And why did you vanish at once away
In the light of a repentant tear?

Anger's Freeing Power

I HAD A dream three walls stood up wherein a raven bird
Against the walls did beat himself and was not this absurd?

For sun and rain beat in that cell that had its fourth wall free
And daily blew the summer shower and the rain came
    presently

And all the pretty summer time and all the winter too
That foolish bird did beat himself till he was black and blue

Rouse up, rouse up, my raven bird, fly by the open wall
You make a prison of a place that is not one at all.

I took my raven by the hand, Oh come, I said, my Raven,
And I will take you by the hand and you shall fly to heaven.

But oh he sobbed and oh he sighed and in a fit he lay
Until two fellow ravens came and stood outside to say:

You wretched bird, conceited lump
You well deserve to pine and thump.

See now a wonder, mark it well
My bird rears up in angry spell,

Oh do I then? he says, and careless flies
O'er flattened wall at once to heaven's skies.

And in my dream I watched him go
And I was glad, I loved him so,

Yet when I woke my eyes were wet
To think Love had not freed my pet

Anger it was that won him hence
As only Anger taught him sense.

Often my tears fall in a shower
Because of Anger's freeing power.

At School
(A Paolo and Francesca situation but more hopeful, say in Purgatory)

At school I always walk with Elwyn
Walk with Elwyn all the day
Oh my darling darling Elwyn
We shall never go away.

This school is a most curious place
Everything happens faintly
And the other boys and girls who are here
We cannot see distinctly.

All the day I walk with Elwyn
And sometimes we also ride
Both of us would always really
Rather be outside.

Most I like to ride with Elwyn
In the early morning sky
Under the solitary mosses
That hang from the trees awry.

The wind blows cold then
And the wind comes to the dawn
And we ride silently
And kiss as we ride down.

Oh my darling darling Elwyn
Oh what a sloppy love is ours
Oh how this sloppy love sustains us
When we get back to the school bars.

There are bars round this school
And inside the lights are always burning bright
And yet there are shadows
That belong rather to the night than to the light.

Oh my darling darling Elwyn
Why is there this dusty heat in this closed school?
All the radiators must be turned full on
Surely that is against the rules?

Hold my hand as we run down the long corridors
Arched over with tombs
We are underground now a long way
Look out, we are getting close to the boiler room.

We are not driven harshly to the lessons you know
That go on under the electric lights
That go on persistently, patiently you might say,
They do not mind if we are not very bright.

Open this door quick, Elwyn, it is break-time
And if we ride quickly we can come to the sea-pool
And swim; will not that be a nice thing to do?
Oh my darling do not look so sorrowful.

Oh why do we cry so much
Why do we not go to some place that is nice?
Why do we only stand close
And lick the tears from each other's eyes?

Darling, my darling
You are with me in the school and in the dead trees' glade
If you were not with me
I should be afraid.

Fear not the ragged dawn skies
Fear not the heat of the boiler room
Fear not the sky where it flies
The jagged clouds in their rusty colour.

Do not tell me not to cry my love
The tears run down your face too
There is still half an hour left
Can we not think of something to do?

There goes the beastly bell
Tolling us to lessons
If I do not like this place much
That bell is the chief reason.

Oh darling Elwyn love
Our tears fall down together
It is because of the place we're in
And because of the weather.

The Occasional Yarrow

It was a mile of greenest grass
Whereon a little stream did pass,
  The Occasional Yarrow

Only in every seventh year
Did this pretty stream appear,
  The Occasional Yarrow

Wading and warbling in its beds
Of grass decked out with daisy heads,
  The Occasional Yarrow

There in my seventh year, and this sweet stream's,
I wandered happily (as happy gleams
  The Occasional Yarrow).

Though now to memory alone
I can call up thy lovely form,
  Occasional Yarrow

I still do bless thy Seventh days
Bless thy sweet name and all who praise
  The Occasional Yarrow.

237

Who is this Who Howls and Mutters?

Who is this that howls and mutters?
It is the Muse, each word she utters
Is thrown against a shuttered door
And very soon she'll speak no more.

Cry louder, Muse, make much more noise
The world is full of rattling toys.
I thought she'd say, Why should I then?
I have spoke low to better men
But oh she did not speak at all but went away
And now I search for her by night and day.

Night and day I seek my Muse
Seek the one I did abuse
She had so sweet a face, so sweet a voice
But oh she did not make sufficient noise.

False plea. I did not listen then
That listen now and listen now in vain.

And still the tale of talent murdered
Untimely and untimely buried
Works in my soul. Forgive me, Lord, I cry
Who only makest Muses howl and sigh
Thou, Lord, repent and give her back to me
Weeping uncomforted, Lord have pity.

He did repent. I have her now again
Howling much worse, and oh the door is open.

Will Man Ever Face Fact and not Feel Flat?

THE rocks and trees in silence stood
To see where Man ran by,
A creature weak as this one is
What can he do but die?
But as they stood and scornful smiled
They heard an angel call:
'The tender creature needeth love,
He needeth love above all.'

This made the rocks and trees laugh more
Until they saw the force of it,
Saw men disembowelling the earth
And killing because of it.

Ah then they found Man admirable,
'But,' said the angel, 'is he?'
And weeping cried, 'The need of love
Makes Man too busy.'

Then God said, 'You are wrong all,
The need of love is meant to call
Man to me, I am love, I,
If it does not, for lack of love he'll die.'

But then came a little wind sneaking along
That was older than all and infamously strong,
'Oh what an artistic animal is our little Man',
Sneered the wind, 'It is wonderful how he can
Invent fairy stories about everything, pit pat,
Will he ever face fact and not feel flat?'

A Dream of Comparison
(After reading Book Ten of 'Paradise Lost')

Two ladies walked on the soft green grass
On the bank of a river by the sea
And one was Mary and the other Eve
And they talked philosophically.

'Oh to be Nothing,' said Eve, 'oh for a
Cessation of consciousness
With no more impressions beating in
Of various experiences.'

'How can Something envisage Nothing?' said Mary,
'Where's your philosophy gone?'
'Storm back through the gates of Birth,' cried Eve,
'Where were you before you were born?'

Mary laughed: 'I love Life,
I would fight to the death for it,
That's a feeling, you say? I will find
A reason for it.'

They walked by the estuary,
Eve and the Virgin Mary,
And they talked until nightfall,
But the difference between them was radical.

A Dream of Nourishment

I HAD a dream of nourishment
Against a breast
My infant face was presst
Ah me the *suffisance* I drew therefrom
What strength, what glory from that fattening fluid,
The fattening most
Was to my infant taste
For oh the sun of strength beat in my veins
And swelled me full, I lay in brightest sun
All ready to put forth, all bursting, all delight.

But in my dream the breast withdrew
In darkness I lay then
And thin,
Thin as a sheeted ghost
And I was famished . . .
Hankered for a dish
I thought, of blood, as in some classicist's
Old tale
To give me hue and substance, make me hale.

Oh breast, oh Best
That I held fast
Oh fattening draught
Timely repast
Quaffed, presst
And lost.

The breast was withdrawn violently
And oh the famishment for me.

Oh What is the Thing He Done?

Oh what is the terrible thing he has done
You are always going on about
My pitiful cousin, my darling one,
That will shut him out from the grace of the sun
Oh what is the thing he done?

Oh it is such a thing as the crocodile
Would shake in each sensitive coil
Oh it is such a thing as would make the blood
Of an adder and his young ones boil
Oh it is a thing as the Prince of Hell
Would plainly declare it was not well.

But what is the thing, oh what is it, pray?
My lips shall never be sullied to say,
Go forth with your cousin, you wretched woman,
And dwell with him in the dark of the sun.

The Choosers

Who shall we send to fetch him away
This young-man Author of the Month of May?
We will send Mr Puff to fetch him away,
We are the Choosers and stand in the way.

Oh we are the Choosers, what we say goes.
Does Puff know this? Yes, Puff knows.
Hey ho what a merry game,
It is as if we were still in Pop, it is the same.

With a hey-ho and a yah
No, we will not have So-and-So
Because we do not like his hat or his Ma.

Outside of this eclectic and up-to-date circle
Slink the sleek Great Ones, and you know
They may go and not care a particle
Because the Angel of Posterity has chosen them
And the Choosers will not be known then,
All the same it is a shame to treat them so.

Let Posterity-Time come
Quick and Choosers be dumb.

Oh why does England cherish her arts in this wise,
Picking inferiorly with grafted eyes?
It is because it is like the school they never forget,
So-and-so must be the driven out one, this the pet.

But Murderous

A MOTHER slew her unborn babe
In a day of recent date
Because she did not wish him to be born in a world
Of murder and war and hate
'Oh why should I bear a babe from my womb
To be broke in pieces by a hydrogen bomb?'

I say this woman deserves little pity
That she was a fool and a murderess
Is a child's destiny to be contained by a mind
That signals only a lady in distress?

And why should human infancy be so superior
As to be too good to be born in this world?
Did she think it was an angel or a baa-lamb
That lay in her belly furled?

Oh the child is the young of its species
Alike with that noble, vile, curious and fierce
How foolish this poor mother to suppose
Her act told us aught that was not murderous

(As, item, That the arrogance of a half-baked mind
Breeds murder; makes us all unkind.)

The Castle

I MARRIED the Earl of Egremont,
I never saw him by day,
I had him in bed at night,
And cuddled him tight.

We had two boys, twins,
Tommy and Roly,
Roly was so fat
We called him Roly-poly.

Oh that was a romantic time,
The castle had such a lonely look,
The estate,
Heavy with cockle and spurge,
Lay desolate.

The ocean waves
Lapped in the castle caves.

Oh I love the ramshackle castle,
And the room
Where our sons were born.

Oh I love the wild
Parkland,
The mild
Sunshine.

Underneath the wall
Sleeps our pet toad,
There the hollyhocks grow tall.

My children never saw their father,
Do not know,
He sleeps in my arms each night
Till cockcrow.

Oh I love the ramshackle castle,
And the turret room
Where our sons were born.

Do Take Muriel Out

Do take Muriel out
She is looking so glum
Do take Muriel out
All her friends are gone.

And after too much pressure
Looking for them in the Palace
She goes home to too much leisure
And this is what her life is.

All her friends are gone
And she is alone
And she looks for them where they have never been
And her peace is flown.

Her friends went into the forest
And across the river
And the desert took their footprints
And they went with a believer.

Ah they are gone they were so beautiful
And she can not come to them
And she kneels in her room at night
Crying, Amen.

Do take Muriel out
Although your name is Death
She will not complain
When you dance her over the blasted heath.

Touch and Go

MAN is coming out of the mountains
But his tail is caught in the pass.
Why does he not free himself
Is he not an ass?

Do not be impatient with him
He is bowed with passion and fret
He is not out of the mountains
He is not half out yet.

Look at his sorrowful eyes
His torn cheeks, his brow
He lies with his head in the dust
Is there no one to help him now?

No, there is no one to help him
Let him get on with it,
Cry the ancient enemies of man
As they cough and spit.

The enemies of man are like trees
They stand with the sun in their branches
Is there no one to help my creature
Where he languishes?

Ah, the delicate creature
He lies with his head in the rubble
Pray that the moment pass
And the trouble.

Look he moves, that is more than a prayer,
But he is so slow
Will he come out of the mountains?
It is touch and go.

The Broken Friendship

'My heart is fallen in despair'
Said Easter Ross to Jolie Bear.
Jolie answered never a word
But passed her plate as if she had not heard.

Mrs Ross is took to her bed
And kept her eye fixed on the bed-rail peg
'When I am dead roll me under the barrow,
And who but pretty Jolie shall carry the harrow.'

Jolie Bear is gone away
Easter Ross's heart is broke,
Everything went out of her
When Jolie never spoke.

Man is a Spirit

Man is a spirit. This the poor flesh knows,
Yet serves him well for host when the wind blows,
Why should this guest go wrinkling up his nose?

I rode with my darling . . .

I RODE with my darling in the dark wood at night
And suddenly there was an angel burning bright
Come with me or go far away he said
But do not stay alone in the dark wood at night.

My darling grew pale he was responsible
He said we should go back it was reasonable
But I wished to stay with the angel in the dark wood at night.

My darling said goodbye and rode off thoughtfully
And suddenly I rode after him and came to a cornfield
Where had my darling gone? Where was the angel now?
The wind bent the corn and drew it along the ground
And the corn said, Do not go alone in the dark wood.

Then the wind drew more strongly and black clouds
      covered the moon
And I rode into the dark wood at night.

There was a light burning in the trees but it was not the angel
And in the pale light stood a tall tower without windows
And a mean rain fell and the voice of the tower spoke,
Do not stay alone in the dark wood at night.

The walls of the pale tower were heavy, in a heavy mood
The great stones stood as if resisting without belief.
Oh how sad sighed the wind, how disconsolately,
Do not ride alone in the dark wood at night.

Loved I once my darling? I love him not now.
Had I a mother beloved? She lies far away.
A sister, a loving heart? My aunt a noble lady?
All all is silent in the dark wood at night.

Mr Over

MR OVER is dead
He died fighting and true
And on his tombstone they wrote
Over to You.

And who pray is this You
To whom Mr Over is gone?
Oh if we only knew that
We should not do wrong.

But who is this beautiful You
We all of us long for so much
Is he not our friend and our brother
Our father and such?

Yes he is this and much more
This is but a portion
A sea-drop in a bucket
Taken from the ocean

So the voices spake
Softly above my head
And a voice in my heart cried: Follow
Where he has led

And a devil's voice cried: Happy
Happy the dead.

God and Man

MAN is my darling, my love and my pain,
My pleasure, my excitement, and my love again,
My wisdom, my courage, my power, my all,
Oh Man, do not come to me until I call.

In man is my life, and in man is my death,
He is my hazard, my pride and my breath,
I sought him, I wrought him, I pant on his worth,
In him I experience indeterminate growth.

Oh Man, Man, of all my animals dearest,
Do not come till I call, though thou weariest first.

Our Bog is Dood

OUR Bog is dood, our Bog is dood,
They lisped in accents mild,
But when I asked them to explain
They grew a little wild.
How do you know your Bog is dood
My darling little child?

We know because we wish it so
That is enough, they cried,
And straight within each infant eye
Stood up the flame of pride,
And if you do not think it so
You shall be crucified.

Then tell me, darling little ones,
What's dood, suppose Bog is?
Just what we think, the answer came,
Just what we think it is.
They bowed their heads. Our Bog is ours
And we are wholly his.

But when they raised them up again
They had forgotten me
Each one upon each other glared
In pride and misery
For what was dood, and what their Bog
They never could agree.

Oh sweet it was to leave them then,
And sweeter not to see,
And sweetest of all to walk alone
Beside the encroaching sea,
The sea that soon should drown them all,
That never yet drowned me.

The Rehearsal

I ALWAYS admire a beautiful woman
And I've brought you some flowers for your beautiful bosom.

The Hat

I LOVE my beautiful hat more than anything
And through my beautiful hat I see a wedding ring
The King will marry me and make me his own before all
And when I am married I shall wear my hat and walk on the
    palace wall.

Wretched Woman
(The child speaks)

WRETCHED woman that thou art
How thou piercest to my heart
With thy misery and graft
And thy lack of household craft.

Lightly Bound
(The mother answers)

You beastly child, I wish you had miscarried,
You beastly husband, I wish I had never married.
You hear the north wind riding fast past the window? He
    calls me.
Do you suppose I shall stay when I can go so easily?

'My beauty was unnoticed.'

Voices about the Princess Anemone

UNDERNEATH the tangled tree
Lies the pale Anemone.

She was the first who ever wrote
The word of fear, and tied it round her throat.

She ran into the forest wild
And there she lay and never smiled.

Sighing, Oh my word of fear
You shall be my only dear.

They said she was a princess lost
To an inheritance beyond all cost.

She feared too much they said, but she says, No,
My wealth is a golden reflection in the stream below.

She bends her head, her hands dip in the water
Fear is a band of gold on the King's daughter.

Human Affection

MOTHER, I love you so.
Said the child, I love you more than I know.
She laid her head on her mother's arm,
And the love between them kept them warm.

Murder

FAREWELL for ever, well for ever fare,
The soul whose body lies beneath this stone!
'Tis easy said by one who had a care
Soul should doff flesh. That has another tone?
My hand brought *Filmer Smith* to this strait bed—
Well, fare his soul well, fear not I the dead.

Poet!

Poet, thou art dead and damned,
That speakst upon no moral text.
I bury one that babbled but;—
Thou art the next. Thou art the next.

*Quand on n'a pas ce que l'on aime, il faut aimer ce que
l'on a—*

Cold as no love, and wild with all negation—
Oh Death in Life, the lack of animation.

Dirge

FROM a friend's friend I taste friendship,
From a friend's friend love,
My spirit in confusion,
Long years I strove,
But now I know that never
Nearer I shall move,
Than a friend's friend to friendship,
To love than a friend's love.

Into the dark night
Resignedly I go,
I am not so afraid of the dark night
As the friends I do not know,
I do not fear the night above
As I fear the friends below.

The Wild Dog

THE City Dog goes to the drinking trough,
He waves his tail and laughs, and goes when he has had
    enough.
His intelligence is on the brink
Of human intelligence. He knows the Council will give him
    a drink.

The Wild Dog is not such an animal,
Untouched by human kind, he is inimical,
He keeps his tail stiff, his eyes blink,
And he goes to the river when he wants a drink.
He goes to the river, he stamps on the mud,
And at night he sleeps in the dark wood.

ORMEROD was deeply troubled
When he read in philosophy and religion
Of man's lust after God,
And the knowledge of God,
And the experience of God
In the achievement of solitary communion and the loss of self.
For he said that he had known this knowledge,
And experienced this experience,
Before life and after death;
But that here in temporal life, and in temporal life only, was
    permitted,
(As in a flaw of divine government, a voluntary recession),
A place where man might impinge upon man,
And be subject to a thousand and one idiotic distractions.
And thus it was that he found himself
Ever at issue with the Schools,
For ever more and more he pursued the distractions,
Knowing them to be ephemeral, under time, peculiar,
And in eternity, without place or puff.
Then, ah then, he said, following the tea-parties,
(And the innumerable conferences for social rearrangement),
I knew, and shall know again, the name of God, closer than
    close;
But now I know a stranger thing,
That never can I study too closely, for never will it come
    again—
Distractions and the human crowd.

I FEAR the ladies and gentlemen under the trees,
Could any of them make an affectionate partner and not
    tease?—
Oh, the affectionate sensitive mind is not easy to please.

Be Off!

I'M sorry to say my dear wife is a dreamer,
And as she dreams she gets paler and leaner.
'Then be off to your Dream, with his fly-away hat,
I'll stay with the girls who are happy and fat.'

The Film Star

DONNEZ à manger aux affamées
It is a film star who passes this way
He is looking so nice the women would like
To have him on a tray
Donnez à manger aux affamées.

The Bottle of Aspirins

'I LOOK at the bottle, when mournful I feel.'
'C'est une ressource contre tout', ajouta-t-il.
(Avec le sombre gaité du pays des suicides
D'où il était)—'two hundred and I am freed,'
He said, 'from anxiety.'

The Devil-my-Wife
(To the tune of 'Golden slumbers')

THE nervous face of my dear wife
Is covered with a fearful grin,
And nods and becks
Come without checks
As the devils pop out and in.

Gush, then, gush and gabble,
Vanity is your dabble,
And in mediocrity
Is your cruelty.

The Smile

WHEN ancient girl is garbed in spite
And turns to rend, and lives to bite,
Oh what can end the marriage night?

Wait, wait, (and with a smile); the dawn
Shall come again, and day return
As fair as any that has gone.

But if the nature of that smile
Be mockery, contempt and guile,
Should such a one my face defile?
No! rather let me *call* her—Crocodile!

Forgot!

THERE is a fearful solitude
Within the careless multitude,
And in the open country too,

He mused, and then it seemed to him
The solitude lay all within;
He longed for some interior din:

Some echo from the worldly rout,
To indicate a common lot,
Some charge that he might be about,
But oh he felt that he was quite forgot.

The White Thought

I SHALL be glad to be silent, Mother, and hear you speak,
You encouraged me to tell too much, and my thoughts are
    weak,
I shall keep them to myself for a time, and when I am older
They will shine as a white worm shines under a green boulder.

In the Night

I LONGED for companionship rather,
But my companions I always wished farther.
And now in the desolate night
I think only of the people I should like to bite.

The Fool

A COUPLE of women is one too many,
Oh, how I wish I could do without any!

The Sliding Mountain

THE terrors of the scenery,
The black rocks of the sliding mountain,
Are hid from the man of family
Who lives beneath the fountain.
His name is Domesticity,
He's married to an ivy tree,
And the little children laugh and scream,
For they do not know what these things mean.

Christmas

A CHILD is born, they cry, a child
And he is Noble and not Mild
(It is the child that makes them wild)

The King sits brooding on his throne
He looks around and calls a man:
My men bring me a heavy stone.

My men bring me a purple robe
And bring me whips and iron goad.
They brought them to him where he strode.

My men bring gold and bring incense
And fetch all noble children at once
That I shall never take offence.

The men fetched the noble children away
They lifted them up and cried: Hurray.
The King sat back and clapped their play.

All noble mild children are brought home
To the wicked King who has cast them down
And ground their bones on the heavy stone.

But the child that is Noble and not Mild
He lies in his cot. He is unbeguiled.
He is Noble, he is not Mild,
And he is born to make men wild.

The Recluse

My soul within the shades of night,
Like a languid plant with a fungoid blight,
Shone out in unearthly damp a bright white light;
Pashy the ground underfoot where I trod,
Musing as I passed of the nature of God,
But on my reverent reveries and fruitful plod
Of tear-strewn steps, like a wrathful rod
Fell the touch of a girl, young in years and officious
Who broke at once at a touch my chain of delicious
Melancholy. Away flew every ecstasy.
With ridiculous intention she drew me to the sun,
My soul's rich languors decried,
And, ere I could chide, away did run,
Leaving my soul undone,
O too much sun, O wretched presumption,
O too little wisdom and too much compunction.

Bog-Face

DEAR little Bog-Face,
Why are you so cold?
And why do you lie with your eyes shut?—
You are not very old.

I am a Child of this World,
And a Child of Grace,
And Mother, I shall be glad when it is over,
I am Bog-Face.

A Man I am

I WAS consumed by so much hate
I did not feel that I could wait,
I could not wait for long at anyrate.
I ran into the forest wild,
I seized a little new-born child,
I tore his throat, I licked my fang,
Just like a wolf. A wolf I am.

I ran wild for centuries
Beneath the immemorial trees,
Sometimes I thought my heart would freeze,
And never know a moment's ease.
But presently the spring broke in
Upon the pastures of my sin,
My poor heart bled like anything.
The drops fell down, I knew remorse,
I tasted that primordial curse,
And falling ill, I soon grew worse.
Until at last I cried on Him,
Before whom angel faces dim,
To take the burden of my sin
And break my head beneath his wing.

Upon the silt of death I swam
And as I wept my joy began
Just like a man. A man I am.

O Happy Dogs of England

O HAPPY dogs of England
Bark well as well you may
If you lived anywhere else
You would not be so gay.

O happy dogs of England
Bark well at errand boys
If you lived anywhere else
You would not be allowed to make such an infernal noise.

Darling Daughters

DARLING daughters, listen to your mother,
I must go away and leave you to each other,
And one shall marry a rich man
And one shall go on an excursion to the Isle of Man
And one shall find her way home if she can.

Death's Ostracism

HE trod in dream upon the brim
Of a deep sea, his mirth too young for him,
For all the people that he smiled upon
Cry: Fool. And they are gone.

With what hostility
And pride
They saw and fled,
He sighed.

The sea ran heavy on a core
Of hidden deep disturbance, ah before
The dream came had an earthquake first
The seabed burst.

Now from the depths
He sees
The sullied waters rise.
All is disease.

And the long reaching waves swing wide,
Sick with death's taste upon the flooding tide,
And dead sea monsters with a deep appal
Of open wounds upon the water sprawl.

His foothold slips.
The clay
Rank with long rains
Gives way.

But falling he will call the waves to friend,
Come cover over all and make an end.
No use, they will not do it, they swing aside.
Death's ostracism in a dream he must abide.

Parrot

THE old sick green parrot
High in a dingy cage
Sick with malevolent rage
Beadily glutted his furious eye
On the old dark
Chimneys of Noel Park

Far from his jungle green
Over the seas he came
To the yellow skies, to the dripping rain,
To the night of his despair.
And the pavements of his street
Are shining beneath the lamp
With a beauty that's not for one
Born under a tropic sun.

He has croup. His feathered chest
Knows no minute of rest.
High on his perch he sits
And coughs and spits,
Waiting for death to come.
Pray heaven it won't be long.

I Hate this Girl

I HATE this girl
She is so cold.
And yet her eyes say
She is not as good as gold.
I should like to kill her,
But what do I do?
Kiss her, kiss her,
And wish that she would kiss me too.

The Cock and the Hen

THE Cock of the North
Has forgotten his worth
And come down south
In a month of drouth.
Woe for the Cock of the North.

The Cock of the Fen
Has forgotten his Hen
Has flown from his pen
And passed out of ken.
Woe for the Cock of the Fen.

The Cock of the North
And the Cock of the Fen
Are one and the same,
And one is the bane
Of the Hen
Of the Cock of the North and the Fen
Who sits in a pen
Of forgotten worth
In a Fen in the North.
Woe for them both.

A Father for a Fool

(To the tune 'Boys and Girls Come out to Play')

LITTLE Master Home-from-School,
This is the Parkland you must rule.
What does it feel like to have a father for a fool?
Your father mortgaged the estate,
Lost his money, blamed fate
And shot himself through the head too late.
There's a father for a fool,
My little Master Home-from-School.

Why does Auntie wear such funny hats
And invert her sentences? Now that's
Positive proof she must be bats.
Why has Parker got all the horses out for me?
Why doesn't Ma meet the train as usually?
Here's hoping they give us shrimps for tea.

Little Master Home-from-School,
Your Ma lies dead, she lies too cool,
She's stone cold dead of a broken heart, the fool.
Jingle-jog the horses go,
And Parker's thinking what I know:
Here comes Master Home-from-School
That had a father for a fool.

Silence and Tears

*'A priestly garment, eminently suitable for conducting funeral
services in inclement weather.'
(From a church outfitter's catalogue)*

THE tears of the widow of the military man
Fell down to the earth as the funeral sentence ran,
Dust to dust, Oh how frightful sighed the mourners as the
    rain began.

But the grave yawned wide and took the tears and the rain,
And the poor dead man was at last free from all his pain,
Pee-wee sang the little bird upon the tree again and again.

Is it not a solemn moment when the last word is said,
And wrapped in cloak of priestly custom we dispose our dead,
And the earth falls heavy, heavy, upon the expensive coffin
    lined with lead?

And may the coffin hold his bones in peace that lies below,
And may the widow woman's tears make a good show,
And may the suitable priestly garment not let the breath of
    scandal through.

For the weather of their happening has been a little inclement,
And would people be so sympathetic if they knew how the story
    went?
Best not put it to the test. Silence and tears are convenient.

To a Dead Vole

Now Vole art dead
And done is all thy bleeding.
Thy soul is sped
And all thy body's heeding
For daily bread
And comfortable bed
Has brought thee where there's no more thought of feeding,
And where the soil is thy last unappreciated quilt.

Noble and Ethereal

NOBLE and ethereal he sped upon his way,
And never Bishop blithe as he about the meadows gay.
He thought upon the Saviour's blood so freely spent for him,
And with a thankful heart he trod above the river's brim,
There for a moment, stood at stare, with meditative eye
He saw within the limpid stream the fishes hurry by,
And all Creation seemed to him a tranquil joyous song
Where never pain had place at all or spite of Ancient Wrong.
He savoured that sweet moment's pause, all Heaven in a day,
And knowing yet his hour not come, he bravely turned away.

Dear Female Heart

DEAR Female Heart, I am sorry for you,
You must suffer, that is all that you can do.
But if you like, in common with the rest of the human race,
You may also look most absurd with a miserable face.

La Gretchen de Nos Jours

WOULD he might come
Again and I
Upon his breast
Again might lie.

Would I had not
In foolish wrath
Driven him ever
From my path.

Would that the sun,
His day's course over,
Might that same day's
Lost dawn recover.

As vain as this
Vain prayer are all
Vain prayers that would
Past days recall.

Never shall sun
Now sunk away
Rise up again
On yesterday.

Never shall love
Untimely slain
Rise from the grave
And live again.

Dear Muse

DEAR Muse, the happy hours we have spent together.
I love you so much in wet or fine weather.
I only wish sometimes you would speak louder,
But perhaps you will do so when you are prouder.
I often think that this will be the next instant,
Meanwhile I am your most obliging confidante.

Gnädiges Fräulein

In the cold light of morning she was looking rather queer,
In the cold light of morning, with a ribbon round her hair,
And her youth lay behind her a long time for many a year.

For when she was young, they took her love away
And sent him to work, beyond the Mexique Bay,
And she thought of him and lost her wits and now her hair is
     gray

With an, 'Oh, if I think of him he'll come again to me,
And an, Oh, it was but a whim that took him o'er the sea;
And an, Oh, for all my eyes are dim they can look lovingly.

'. . . and the clouds return after the rain'
(To the tune 'Worthy the Lamb')

In a shower of tears I sped my fears
And lost my heavy pain,
But now my grief that knew relief
Is sultried o'er again.

Of leaf and flower of that first shower
No memories remain.
The clouds hang down in heavy frown
But still it does not rain.

Happy the man of simple span
Whose cry waits on his pain,
But there are some whose mouths are dumb
When the clouds return again.

Out of Time

IT is a formal and deserted garden
With many a flower bed and winding path.
A cupid stands and draws a bow at venture
Upon a marble bath.

All round his feet the eager ivy grows,
Stretches upon the stone, above the ground,
And in the ivy flowers the busy bee
Makes a melodious sound.

The air is languorous with summer scents
And still it lies upon the garden all
As still and secret as it stayed upon
A funeral.

The sun shines brightly in the upper air
And casts his beams upon the garden grass.
There spilled they lie a carpet of dull gold
Where shadows pass.

The garden gives to these primaeval beams
That strew its floor a plastered yellow tone
As of too mellow sunshine that brings on
A thunder stone.

It is an ominous enchanted garden
That can transmogrify the healthful rays,
Can hold and make them an essential part
Of unquiet days.

Ah me, the unquiet days they tread me down,
The hours and minutes beat upon my head.
I have spent here the time of three men's lives
And am not dead.

And even as I count the days that pass
I lose the total and begin again.
It is an evil garden out of Time
A place of pain.

The Children of the Cross

OH cold and ferocious are the children of the cross,
They have captured us and bound us and their gain is our
    loss.
But straining to death
In the stench of the fire's breath
We leave lonely for ever the children of the cross.

Look, Look

HE flies so high
Upon the sky
Like winged piggywig
Above his sty.

The sky is
Too high for you. Is
Not the world
A good sty for you?

Ceux qui luttent . . .

CEUX qui luttent ce sont ceux qui vivent.
And down here they luttent a very great deal indeed.
But if life be the desideratum, why grieve, ils vivent.

The Photograph

THEY photographed me young upon a tiger skin
And now I do not care at all for kith and kin,
For oh the tiger nature works within.

Parents of England, not in smug
Fashion fancy set on a rug
Of animal fur the darling you would hug,

For lately born is not too young
To scent the savage he sits upon,
And tiger-possessed abandon all things human.

Little Boy Sick

I AM not God's little lamb
I am God's sick tiger.
And I prowl about at night
And what most I love I bite,
And upon the jungle grass I slink,
Snuff the aroma of my mental stink,
Taste the salt tang of tears upon the brink
Of my uncomfortable muzzle.
My tail my beautiful, my lovely tail,
Is warped.
My stripes are matted and my coat once sleek
Hangs rough and undistinguished on my bones.
O God I was so beautiful when I was well,
My heart, my lungs, my sinews and my reins
Consumed a solitary ecstasy,
And light and pride informed each artery.
Then I a temple, now a charnel house,
Then I a high hosannah, now a dirge,
Then I a recompense of God's endeavour,
Now a reproach and earnest of lost toil.
Consider, Lord, a tiger's melancholy
And heed a minished tiger's muted moan,
For thou art sleek and shining bright
And I am weary.
Thy countenance is full of light
And mine is dreary.

'It was I!'

Egocentric

WHAT care I if good God be
If he be not good to me,
If he will not hear my cry
Nor heed my melancholy midnight sigh?
What care I if he created Lamb,
And golden Lion, and mud-delighting Clam,
And Tiger stepping out on padded toe,
And the fecund earth the Blindworms know?
He made the Sun, the Moon and every Star,
He made the infant Owl and the Baboon,
He made the ruby-orbèd Pelican,
He made all silent inhumanity,
Nescient and quiescent to his will,
Unquickened by the questing conscious flame
That is my glory and my bitter bane.
What care I if Skies are blue,
If God created Gnat and Gnu,
What care I if good God be
If he be not good to me?

Alfred the Great

Honour and magnify this man of men
Who keeps a wife and seven children on £2 10
Paid weekly in an envelope
And yet he never has abandoned hope.

How far can you Press a Poet?

How far can you press a poet?
To the last limit and he'll not show it
And one step further and he's dead
And his death is upon your head.

Night-Time in the Cemetery

THE funeral paths are hung with snow
About the graves the mourners go
To think of those who lie below.
The churchyard pales are black against the night
And snow hung here seems doubly white.
I have a horror of this place
A horror of each moonlit mourner's face
These people are not familiar
But strange and stranger than strange peculiar
They have that look of a cheese do you know sour-sweet
You can smell their feet.
Yet must I tread
About my dead
And guess the forms within the grave
And hear the clank of jowl on jowl
Where low lies kin no love could save.
Yet stand I by my grave as they by theirs. Oh bitter Death
That brought their love and mine unto a coffin's breadth.

Alone in the Woods

ALONE in the woods I felt
The bitter hostility of the sky and the trees
Nature has taught her creatures to hate
Man that fusses and fumes
Unquiet man
As the sap rises in the trees
As the sap paints the trees a violent green
So rises the wrath of Nature's creatures
At man
So paints the face of Nature a violent green.
Nature is sick at man
Sick at his fuss and fume
Sick at his agonies
Sick at his gaudy mind
That drives his body
Ever more quickly
More and more
In the wrong direction.

Es war einmal

I RAISED my gun
I took the sight
Against the sun
I shot a kite.

I raised my gun
I took the sight
A second one
I shot in flight.

I raised my gun
I shot a plover
I loaded up
And shot another.

Now round about me
Lay the dead
One more, one more,
Then home to bed.

Pray Heaven, said I
Send the best
That ever took
Lead to its breast.

Upon the word
Upon the right
Rose up a phoenix
Beaming bright.

I raised my gun
I took the sight
My lead unbarred
That breast of white,

Alas for awful
Magic art
The bullet bounced
Into my heart.

The phoenix bled
My heart can not
But heavy sits
'Neath leaden shot.

Leave shooting, friend,
Or if you must
Shoot only what
Is mortal dust.

Pray not to Heaven
He stock your bag
Or you may feel
Your vitals sag.

Pray not to Heaven
For heavenly bird
Or Heaven may take you
At your word.

Infant

IT was a cynical babe
Lay in its mother's arms
Born two months too soon
After many alarms
Why is its mother sad
Weeping without a friend?
Where is its father—say?
He tarries in Ostend.
It was a cynical babe. Reader before you condemn, pause,
It was a cynical babe. Not without cause.

Dream

I CAME upon it in a dream
It was a sad and mournful scene
A mournfuller could not have been.

I rode my steed upon a plain
Against a bitter driving rain
So may I never ride again.

No man was there I rode alone
The icy wind cut to the bone
I came upon a funeral stone.

Deep in a yew tree grove it stood
And on its side were marks of blood
And at its foot the yellow mud.

I left the saddle, left my steed,
I went down on my hands to read
The tombstone's closely written screed;——

But oh from left and oh from right
Rang out a voice of ghostly might:
'Leave, lady, leave thy Leda light!'

The rain fell down with heavy stroke,
I mounted up, my heart was broke.
I turned about and I awoke.

The Bereaved Swan

WAN
Swan
On the lake
Like a cake
Of soap
Why is the swan
Wan
On the lake?
He has abandoned hope.

Wan
Swan
On the lake afloat
Bows his head:
O would that I were dead
For her sake that lies
Wrapped from my eyes
In a mantle of death,
The swan saith.

Bag-Snatching in Dublin

SISLEY
Walked so nicely
With footsteps so discreet
To see her pass
You'd never guess
She walked upon the street.

Down where the Liffey waters' turgid flood
Churns up to greet the ocean-driven mud,
A bruiser in a fix
Murdered her for 6/6.

The River Deben

ALL the waters of the river Deben
Go over my head to the last wave even
Such a death were sweet to seven times seven.

Death sits in the boat with me
His face is shrouded but he smiles I see
The time is not yet, he will not come so readily.

But he smiles and I smile it is pleasant in the boat at night
There is no moon rising but from the east a light
Shines in the sky, is it dawn or dawn's twilight?

Over here the waters are dark as a deep chasm
Shadowed by cliffs of volcanic spasm
So dark so dark is the waves' fashion.

But the oars dip I am rowing they dip and scatter
The phosphorescence in a sudden spatter
Of light that is more actual than a piece of matter.

Up the Deben we row I row towards Waldringfield
It is a long way yet, my arms ache but will not yield
In this physical tiredness there is a happy shield.

Oh happy Deben, oh happy night, and night's companion
        Death,
What exultation what ecstasy is in thy breath
It is as salt as the salt silt that lies beneath.

Flow tidal river flow, draw wind from the east,
Smile pleasant Death, smile Death in darkness blessed,
But tarry day upon the crack of dawn. Thou comest unwished.

Never Again

NEVER again will I weep
And wring my hands
And beat my head against the wall
Because
Me nolentem fata trahunt
But
When I have had enough
I will arise
And go unto my Father
And I will say to Him:
Father, I have had enough.

Little Boy Lost

THE wood was rather old and dark
The witch was very ugly
And if it hadn't been for father
Walking there so smugly
I never should have followed
The beckoning of her finger.
Ah me how long ago it was
And still I linger
Under the ever interlacing beeches
Over a carpet of moss
I lift my hand but it never reaches
To where the breezes toss
The sun-kissed leaves above.
The sun?
Beware.
The sun never comes here.
Round about and round I go
Up and down and to and fro
The woodlouse hops upon the tree
Or should do but I really cannot see.
Happy fellow. Why can't I be
Happy as he?
The wood grows darker every day
It's not a bad place in a way
But I lost the way
Last Tuesday
Did I love father, mother, home?
Not very much; but now they're gone
I think of them with kindly toleration
Bred inevitably of separation.
Really if I could find some food
I should be happy enough in this wood
But darker days and hungrier I must spend
Till hunger and darkness make an end.

What is the Time?
or
St. Hugh of Lincoln

WHAT is the time, my limber lad,
What is the time, I pray?
I am old and blind
And weak in my mind,
But what is the time of day?

He took the youth by his golden hair
He dragged him up a crooked stair
Never more was *Hughie* seen,
Be warned, my child, while the grass is green.

Major Macroo

MAJOR Hawkaby Cole Macroo
Chose
Very wisely
A patient Griselda of a wife with a heart of gold
That never beat for a soul but him
Himself and his slightest whim.

He left her alone for months at a time
When he had to have a change
Just had to
And his pension wouldn't stretch to a fare for two
And he didn't want it to.

And if she wept she was game and nobody knew it
And she stood at the edge of the tunnel and waved as his
      train went through it.

And because it was cheaper they lived abroad
And did he care if she might be unhappy or bored?
He did not.
He'd other things to think of—a lot.

He'd fads and he fed them fat,
And she could lump it and that was that.

He'd several boy friends
And she thought it was nice for him to have them,
And she loved him and felt that he needed her and waited
And waited and never became exasperated.

Even his room
Was dusted and kept the same,
And when friends came
They went into every room in the house but that one
Which Hawkaby wouldn't have shown.

Such men as these, such selfish cruel men
Hurting what most they love what most loves them,
Never make a mistake when it comes to choosing a woman
To cherish them and be neglected and not think it inhuman.

All Things Pass

ALL things pass
Love and mankind is grass.